IDOLS OF THE PEOPLE
Miniature Images of Clay
in the Ancient Near East

Idols of the People
Miniature Images of Clay in the Ancient Near East

P. R. S. Moorey
Department of Antiquities, Ashmolean Museum
Oxford

THE SCHWEICH LECTURES
OF THE BRITISH ACADEMY
2001

Published for THE BRITISH ACADEMY
by OXFORD UNIVERSITY PRESS

Oxford University Press, Great Clarendon Street, Oxford OX2 6DP

Oxford New York
Auckland Bangkok Bogotá Buenos Aires Cape Town Chennai
Dar es Salaam Delhi Hong Kong Istanbul Karachi Kolkata
Kuala Lumpur Madrid Melbourne Mexico City Mumbai Nairobi
São Paulo Shanghai Singapore Taipei Tokyo Toronto

© The British Academy 2003
Database right The British Academy (maker)
First published 2003

All rights reserved. No part of this publication may be reproduced,
stored in a retrieval system, or transmitted, in any form or by any means,
without the prior permission in writing of the British Academy,
or as expressly permitted by law, or under terms agreed with the appropriate
reprographics rights organization. Enquiries concerning reproduction
outside the scope of the above should be sent to the Publications Department,
The British Academy, 10 Carlton House Terrace, London SW1Y 5AH

You must not circulate this book in any other binding or cover
and you must impose this same condition on any acquirer

British Library Cataloguing in Publication Data
Data available

ISBN 0–19–726280–5

Typeset in Times
by J & L Composition, Filey, North Yorkshire
Printed in Great Britain
on acid-free paper by
CPI Bath

Contents

List of Plates	vii
Preface	ix
Acknowledgements	x

I. In the Beginning: Origins and Originating questions
  1. Terracottas and Old Testament study — 1
  2. Two paradigm shifts in recent scholarship: in the origins of Israelite religion and in cognitive archaeology — 3
  3. Some conceptual hazards: toys; magic; fertility — 7
  4. Clay and cuneiform texts: inscribed terracottas in ancient Mesopotamia — 11
  5. Images and imagery: the value of broad and extended perspectives — 13
  6. Contrasting terracotta repertories: Canaan, Israel and Judah — 14
  7. Some primary considerations — 15

II. Terracottas in Early Complex Societies: Sumer, Babylonia, Syria, Egypt and Canaan (*c.* 3000–1150 BC)
  1. Contrasts in the terracotta imagery of Canaan, Israel and Judah — 23
  2. The emergence of nude female images in early urban societies in Sumer, (c. 3000–2100 BC) — 25
  3. The 'Nude Female' in Babylonia (c. 2100–1650 BC) — 28
  4. The migration of the one-piece open-mould technology to Syria — 34
  5. Terracotta imagery in Canaan and the Egyptian connection — 35
  6. Terracotta Plaques in Canaan during the Late Bronze Age (c. 1650–1150 BC) — 37
  7. The Canaanite terracotta legacy in the first millennium BC (Iron Age). — 40

III.	**Terracotta Imagery in Israel and Judah under the Divided Monarchy (*c.* 925–586 BC)**	
	1. Israelite goddesses: terracotta figurines	47
	2. The Emergence of free-standing Terracottas in Israel and Judah	50
	3. Two key contexts: Cave 1 (Ophel) in Jerusalem (Judah) and area E-257 in Samaria (Israel)	52
	4. The repertory of Judean terracottas in the eighth and seventh Centuries BC	58
	5. Closing comments	67
Abbreviations		69
Bibliography		70
Index		79

List of Plates

Between pages 20 and 21
1. Handmade seated female terracotta with painted details (the so-called 'Mother Goddess' type); excavated at Chagar Bazar, Syria; Halaf Period, c. 5500–5000 BC; 10 cm high. (1936.90).
2. Inscribed handmade terracotta guardian dog; excavated at Kish in Iraq; seventh to sixth century BC; 6.7 cm high. (1924.302).
3. Inscribed handmade terracotta 'bitch' (as inscription); excavated at Kish in Iraq; c. 2000 BC; 5 cm long (1931.67).
4. Handmade 'Mother Goddess handles' from pottery storage jars; excavated at Kish ('Cemetery A') in Iraq; c. 2500 BC; 8 cm, 8 cm, 7.6 cm high (1925.163, 166, 167).

Between pages 44 and 45
5 a,b. Two handmade terracotta suppliants or worshippers; excavated at Kish in Iraq; c. 2100 BC; 7.6 cm, 8.6 cm (1927.3282; 1931.163).
6. Babylonian terracotta mouldmade plaque of the upper part of a deity or her cult image; source unknown; c. 1900–1750 BC; 10 cm high. (1949.920).
7. Babylonian terracotta mouldmade plaque of a nude female standing on a podium; source unknown; c. 1900–1750 BC; 12 cm high (1924.499).
8. Mouldmade terracotta model bed with reclining nude female; perhaps from southwest Iran; c. 1500–1200 BC; 13 cm long (1965.757).
9. Handmade Syrian Nude Female terracotta figurine with gold ear-rings and navel plug; source unknown; late third to early second millennium BC; 15.3 cm long (1933.1182).
10. Mouldmade terracotta 'Qudshu' plaque; from Gezer in Israel; c. 1300 BC; 12 cm long (1912.621).
11. Mouldmade blue glass pendant in the shape of an 'Astarte' plaque; excavated at Tell ed-Duweir (Lachish) in Israel; 5.5 cm long (1955.501). (Print from original excavation negative).
12. Handmade terracotta female 'pillar-figurines'; from various sites in Syria; seventh century BC; 13.5 cm; 10.3 cm; 13.9 cm; 12.5 cm high (1913.447; 1913.634; 1914.795; 1914.796).

Between pages 68 and 69

13. Handmade terracotta horsemen figurines; from sites in Syria (centre) and Amathus in Cyprus (sides); seventh to fifth centuries BC; 12.4 cm; 14.2 cm; 12.2 cm; 13.5 cm high (C.262; 1913.648; 1914.872; C.261).
14. Terracotta Judean female pillar-figurine; said to be from a tomb at Bethlehem; seventh century BC; 17.5 cm high (British Museum 93091).
15. Terracotta horse and rider (note the extent of damage); excavated from Cave I at Jerusalem (Ophel); seventh century BC; 10.5 cm high (horse); 5.4 cm high (man) (1968.1384; 1968.1386).
16. Terracotta model of a building (note extent of damage); excavated from Cave I at Jerusalem (Ophel); seventh century BC; 8.8 × 7 cm (1968.1404).

All, except Plate 14, are published by courtesy of the Visitors of the Ashmolean Museum, Oxford; Plate 14 is published by courtesy of the Trustees of the British Museum. The numbers give in brackets are the museum accession numbers.

Preface

The scholar invited to be the Schweich Lecturer is required to give three lectures in succession in anticipation of their eventual publication. It is, then, necessary in their composition to accommodate the needs both of an audience, whose members may well not be the same on all three occasions, and eventually, it is hoped, of readers, who are more likely to treat them as a continuous text in three consecutive chapters. The readers, however, will not have the assistance of the long sequence of illustrations provided by lantern-slides for the lecture audiences. No compromise is entirely satisfactory; but it is hoped enough illustration is offered here to avoid obscurity. The three lectures were conceived as *essays*, self-contained up-to-a-point, yet thematically linked in ways that should allow them to be intelligible alone or in combination.

These Schweich Lectures set out to investigate the social contexts, of which any religious aspect is but a part, of the popular terracotta imagery of Canaan, Israel and Judah within its wider Near Eastern context. These miniature images are treated here as a distinctive phenomenon with prehistoric antecedents and recurrent characteristics across millennia. They are amongst the most frequently cited objects of cultic significance from local excavations, more often found elsewhere than in official shrines and temples.

Acknowledgements

I would like to express my sincere thanks to the members of the Schweich Committee for the great honour they did me in inviting me to give the Schweich Lectures for 2001. I am also particularly indebted to the Director and Visitors of the Ashmolean Museum, Oxford, for granting me eleven months sabbatical leave from September 2000 to August 2001 to complete a *catalogue raisonné* of the ancient Near Eastern Terracotta in the Museum. It generated the theme and much of the content of these lectures. The bibliography makes clear my debts to many scholars in related fields of study, not least those far from archaeology.

I first encountered battered and broken Judean Pillar Figurines in 1963, as a very junior site-supervisor on the late Dame Kathleen Kenyon's excavations in Jerusalem. I worked then far down the slopes of Ophel in an area where some years later the assemblage of figurines in Cave I described in lecture 3, were found. This stimulated an interest in terracottas renewed, in a very different setting, by participation in Nicholas Postgate's excavations at Abu Salabikh in Iraq in the 1981 season when, as registrar, I helped to retrieve by water sieving some of the numerous, often fragmentary, terracottas of the Early Dynastic Period found in the '6G Ash-Tip' (McAdam 1993). In the interval I had made a special study of the terracottas from the Oxford-Field Museum, Chicago Expedition to Kish in Iraq, 1923–1933, with the much appreciated assistance of the staff of the National Museum of Antiquities in Baghdad and various Directors of the Field Museum, Chicago. I am also particularly indebted to curators, past and present, of the Rockefeller Museum and the Israel Museum in Jerusalem for access over the years to objects and information imperceptibly absorbed into these lectures.

The staff of the British Academy sustained me before, during and after the delivery of the lectures in various ways for which I am most grateful. I am particularly indebted in the Ashmolean Museum to Mrs Suzanne Anderson who provided invaluable secretarial support throughout and to Mrs Julie Clements, Mr Keith Bennett and the members of the Ashmolean's photographic studio who aided me with the illustrations.

P. R. S. Moorey

'The uneasy thought that actual religious practice in ancient Israel might not have mirrored our texts in any recognizable fashion has disturbed many a scholar's ponderings. Yet it must be admitted, little seems to have been done about the problem except to strive to mine the biblical mother lode yet deeper'

Holladay 1987, 249

I

In the Beginning:
Origins and Originating Questions

1. Terracottas and Old Testament study

The Schweich Lecturer is required by the Trust, established in 1907 by his daughter in memory of Mr. Leopold Schweich of Paris, to further 'research into the archaeology, art, history, languages and literature of Ancient Civilizations with reference to Biblical Study'. As an archaeologist I have read these terms of reference as a challenge to address a topic for which material culture provides evidence absent from the literary tradition, however enigmatic such evidence might prove to be. It is well known that a substantial amount of what is loosely called cult or ritual equipment revealed by excavations in the area of modern Israel and Palestine cannot be connected with any reference in the Hebrew Bible. This is to be expected from accounts written by religious reformers who were describing the Israelite religion they advocated rather than as practised in their time. Moreover, not only is the account idealistic, it is élitist in its concern with established religion not with the religious practices of the majority of the population within their families and in their homes (cf. Dever 2001: 173–187).

Much of this common paraphernalia is made of clay, the material most readily available to the greatest number of people. Miniature clay images of anthropomorphic, zoomorphic and inanimate forms are conspicuous amongst them. They follow a tradition of image-making amongst ordinary people that is evident in the Near East from the time of the earliest village settlements there some ten thousand years ago. Indeed, clay figurines appeared before pottery was manufactured and remained in production beyond the time covered by the Old Testament.

Amongst artefacts regularly cited as having cultic significance in reports of excavations in those regions occupied by Canaan, Israel and Judah in antiquity clay figurines are the commonest (cf. Fowler 1985: 333). Although there were such images which did service to public cults, the excavation of a clay figurine in this region is not necessarily any indication that the find spot had been a place of official or public worship. Over fifty years ago James Pritchard (1943: 87) convincingly demonstrated that they were 'to judge from frequency of their appearance, the property of private houses rather than merely confined to places connected exclusively with cult'. Subsequent discoveries have not seriously challenged this generalization.

The imagery and rituals of ordinary people in their homes and places of work remain among the more important and elusive unknowns in the ideologies of the ancient Near East, as they generally fall outside the range of written records, even where they have survived, as in Iraq. Miniature images of anthropomorphic, zoomorphic and, much more rarely, of inanimate subjects, such as buildings, furniture and vehicles, constitute virtually the only body of material evidence for them that is recurrently, to varying degrees, available over a period of some eight thousand years.

Significantly, they were generally treated like any other household rubbish once they had served their purpose. It is primary contexts, preferably closed ones, and the association of objects in them, that are crucial in archaeological practice to any attempts to understand function. Consequently, the fact that excavators should so often have recovered terracottas from contexts of disposal rather than of use has been a severe restraint on their proper study.

Investigation of the roles of such miniature clay images in Old Testament Studies, when they have not been dismissed out-of-hand as no more than children's toys, has more often than not been narrowly focused, chronologically, geographically and typologically. Female anthropomorphic images dominate the relevant literature, even when they are recurrently associated in excavations with miniatures of males, of animals and birds, and of objects of daily use. This is particularly true of those recovered from excavations in the settlements of Israel and Judah at the time of the Divided Monarchy (*c*. 925–586 BC).

These lectures, whose primary intention is to open the subject up, takes the opposite approach. They embody three working assumptions:

First, that any agenda for investigating terracotta figurines in Canaan, Israel and Judah, must now take account of the aims and methods of parallel inquiries across prehistoric and early historic cultures in the Near East and elsewhere in the ancient world.

Second, that a basic understanding of their antecedents, combined with an over-view of contemporary figurine production in regions adjacent to the 'Holy Land', is a prerequisite for any attempt to elucidate their potentially diverse and still elusive roles in the daily lives of the ordinary people who in general made, used and often randomly disposed of them.

Third, that such clay miniatures when recurrently found together, in all their variety, even in rubbish deposits, were originally constituents of a single system of symbols. Any attempts to understand the functions and meanings of one type, or trait, however predominant in a particular context, must to avoid distortion take them all into account in the final analysis. It is this configuration that offers the best hope of elucidating the roles of any particular type.

2. Two paradigm shifts in recent scholarship: in the origins of Israelite religion and in congnitive archaeology

My choice of this subject was much influenced by recent paradigm shifts in scholarship in the two fields of study most directly involved: Old Testament Studies on the one hand, Archaeology on the other. Both these shifts require brief introductions to make the potential for interrelating them in this case evident from the outset.

Research on the formative stage of Israelite Religion has recently exhibited both a new emphasis on its diversity and a fresh recognition of what it had shared with the religions of its neighbours in so far as they were all, to a greater or lesser extent, heirs to the cultural traditions of the region. For so long as Biblical scholarship was primarily concerned with endorsing the uniqueness of Israelite religion, pluralistic elements in its early cult practices were disregarded or minimized. The change of emphasis may not have been created, but it was certainly accelerated by the remarkable coincidence of the discovery of two particular eighth century BC inscriptions in modern Israel, one in the later 1960s, the other in the mid. 1970s. The first was extracted from a rock-cut pillar in a burial cave near Khirbet el-Qom, 12 kilometres west of Hebron (cf. Dever 1999). The other was inscribed, in association with drawings, on a pottery jar found during controlled excavations in what may have been a shrine in the gateway to a fort at Kuntillet ʿAjrud, about fifty kilometres south of Kadesh-Banea in northern Sinai (cf. Meshel 1978; 1979), where support beams have yielded calibrated Carbon-14 dates been 830 and 760 BC. Both inscriptions include the phrase 'Yahweh (and) his *aserah*' (cf. Hadley 2000: 84–152), implying some type of relationship between God of the Old Testament and one of the best known of Canaanite goddesses (cf. Day 2000).

In the quarter of a century of discussion following this second discovery, considerable attention has been paid to whether the word asherah (*'ăšērâ*) here refers directly to the Goddess as the partner of Yahweh or to her wooden cult symbol, a pole or tree as in *Deuteronomy* 16: 21: 'You shall not plant any tree as an *asherah* beside the altar of the Lord your God which you shall make' (cf. Hestrin 1987). Whatever the case, these inscriptions indicate the vitality of a popular cult of Asherah in the eighth to seventh centuries BC.

Evident in the paradigm shift in Old Testament scholarship is an increased general willingness to introduce material remains into the body of evidence advanced for consideration. Amongst the *realia* drawn into the debate over these two inscriptions are a group of terracotta female figurines, with a distinctive columnar body shape, dating to the same period. From their shape and primary area of distribution they have become known as the 'Judean Pillar Figurines (JPFs)' (cf. Kletter 1996) amongst archaeologists, but more commonly now in Old Testament studies as 'figurines of the goddess Asherah' (Day 2000: 227). If fragments are taken into account, many thousands are already recorded. Indeed, this statistic is increasingly cited as evidence for the popularity of the cult of Asherah at the time of the United Monarchy, at least in Judah.

Raz Kletter's monograph of 1996, *The Judean Pillar-Figurines and the Archaeology of Asherah,* assembled and critically assessed the primary data, leading him to conclude that these terracottas are 'indeed a representation of Biblical Asherah: this is the simplest and most logical explanation ... but it is not proven and should not be taken for granted' (Kletter 1996: 81). Judith Hadley, who did not have access to Kletter's monograph when writing her recent detailed and judicious, *The Cult of Asherah in Ancient Israel and Judah: Evidence for a Hebrew Goddess* (2000), concluded that 'the exaggerated breasts emphasize the nurturing aspect of the mother goddess, but as other symbols of divinity are lacking, it is impossible to determine for certain what deity is intended. Nevertheless these figurines maybe smaller copies of the asherah poles ... there is no evidence, however, to suggest these ... are the objects to which the Chronicler refers as "asherim"' (Hadley 2000: 204–5). Neither scholar investigated whether they might represent women as worshippers or suppliants. Nor did either scholar fully weigh up the implications of the unusual presence of a male component in the repertory of terracottas in Judah at this time in seeking the meaning and function of the female pillar figurines. Moreover, the place of these female images in the wider world of terracotta production and use in the Near East at the time remains equally unexplored. Such issues will be the concern of the third lecture, whilst the second will deal with their Canaanite precursors and their legacy.

At almost the same time as the *asherah* question was engaging the attention of Old Testament scholars, a paradigm shift in archaeology saw a renewed readiness, after a generation fiercely averse to using archaeological data for such purposes, to investigate 'the spiritual preoccupations of prehistory' (Goodison and Morris 1998: 10), sometimes more generally termed cognitive archaeology.

The systematic deconstruction of the potent nineteenth century hypothesis of a Universal Earth or Morther Goddess in antiquity has been one of the most evident aspects of this paradigm shift. A generation ago Raphael Patai in his pioneering study *The Hebrew Goddess* (1967), still owed much to this hypothesis of a universal longing for the ultimate mother when he argued that there had always been a Hebrew Goddess beside the Hebrew God. More recent treatments of Asherah and her iconography still commonly refer to this idea. This is independent of the fact that Asherah (Athirat) in the Late Bronze Age texts from Ugarit (Ras Shamra) was El's consort and variously described as 'creatress, mistress, or mother' of the gods (Hadley 2000: 39).

The enduring attraction of the 'Mother Goddess' (Plate 1) hypothesis owes much to progressive simplification of Johann Jacob Bachofen's original concept. He is now the least famous member of a trio of scholars, who together with Burckhardt and Nietzsche, brought enduring fame to the then tiny university of Basle in Switzerland in the third quarter of the nineteenth century (cf. Gossman 2000). Bachofen, best known for his *Mutterrecht (Matriarchy)* of 1861, which he spent many years rewriting and never finished, sought just before the birth of modern prehistoric archaeology to reach back to a stage in the human past important for three things: the domination of religion; a sense of death identical with a recognition of life; and the significance of women in life, death and religion as mothers, as determinants of the social order, and as symbols not only of birth but also of death. His knowledge of the ancient Near East, inevitably at the time, was derived almost entirely from the literature of ancient Greece and Rome, particularly in so far as it related to the mythology of ancient Turkey.

Over a century later, during the nineteen-sixties, it was no accident that James Mellaart (1967), when explaining his famous and remarkable finds of the Neolithic Period at Çatalhöyuk in Central Turkey, in the words of Bachofen's most influential disciple in our time, Jacques Cauvin (2000: 92): 'quite rightly underlined the funerary association of this imagery, the Mistress of Life also ruling the Dead'. This last aspect is often overlooked. Indeed, so powerful has Bachofen's legacy been that substantial critical appraisals of it, when applied to terracotta imagery, such as Peter Ucko's study of *Anthropomorphic Figurines of Predynastic Egypt and Neolithic Crete* (1968), which made extensive use of anthropological data, had to wait a generation to receive due attention (cf. Ucko 1996). The reason for this in ancient Near Eastern Studies is in part to be attributed to the rarity, at that time, of any real dialogue between archaeologists and specialists in the ancient languages of the region. Now that the Mother Goddess hypothesis is increasingly confronted by scholars familiar with these languages, the individuality of the many goddesses (and gods) of the region in antiquity is particularly made evident and emphasized to confound this reductionist conception (cf. Westenholz 1998).

Central to the most recent research on prehistoric terracottas, as to Ucko's approach, has been an emphasis on the explanatory value of arguing from parallel cases in the literature of anthropology and ethnography. The strength of this approach, judiciously applied, is that it alerts archaeologists to potential questions beyond the range of their experience of the real world and of their professional reading. Indeed, it fortifies the position taken by R.G. Collingwood, the only distinguished philosopher who was also a field archaeologist, that in studying the past it is the questions that really matter since they can never be fixed. 'My work in archaeology,' he wrote in 1939, 'impressed upon me the importance of the "questioning activity"' (Collingwood 1939: 30). But, of course, it does not follow that such parallel cases also provide the methods. Archaeologists too often lack the necessary evidence and are always without the informants usually taken for granted by anthropologists in the field.

In Near Eastern archaeology Mary Voigt's (1983) publication of the terracottas she found during her excavation of a prehistoric village at Hajji Firuz Tepe in northwest Iran a generation ago, includes the most valuable appraisal of Ucko's conclusions, which are at the heart of her discussion, in the light of direct field experience. She (Voigt 1983: 186; cf. recently Voigt 2000) endorsed his five primary functional categories: 1: *cult figurines*, or representations of supernatural beings used primarily as symbols or objects of worship; 2: *vehicles of magic* (regarded as symbiotic with religion, not antagonistic to it) which are manipulated and in many cases disposed of as a key element in rituals intended to produce, prevent or reverse a specific situation. These may range from the insurance of fertility (for humans and animals as well as crops), to the protection of health or property and the prevention of natural disasters; 3: *didactic or teaching aids*; 4 *representations of living or dead people (ancestors)*; and 5: *toys*. This remains a sound basis for appraisal of all the categories of terracotta imagery to be considered here.

Throughout this inquiry the meaning of particular miniature forms, anthropomorphic, zoomorphic and inanimate, and their mediating role in the daily lives of those who made and used them, will be the recurrent issues. The primary value of anthropological research on figurines for present purposes is twofold. *In the first place* it highlights the fact that figurines of similar appearance may have represented different beings, natural or supernatural; that the same type of figurine might have multiple functions; and that in one assemblage the same type might have had more than one function. *In the second place*, it indicates that terracotta anthropomorphic figurines do not have to conform to the tendency to regard them as necessarily representative of supernatural beings common in ancient Near Eastern studies. In the levels of society primarily involved here, the uses of terracotta figurines at times embraced functions where in modern literate societies writing would be the more familiar medium. They may have embodied aspects of prevailing ideologies, whilst also reflecting contemporary society by encoding varieties of ritually significant knowledge relevant to the world of man and nature.

3. Some conceptual hazards: toys; magic; fertility

A potential role as toys for terracotta figurines serves as an excellent introduction to the ambiguities and complexities of this subject. It is vital to be recurrently mindful of the cultural filters through which modern thinking about it passes (cf. Westenholz 1998). This is one of them. After his pioneer excavations at Tell Beit Mirsim, southeast of Tell ed-Duweir (Lachish), some seventy years ago, Albright (1943) devoted a whole section of his report on the excavations to a discussion of the terracotta figurines he had found under the rubric: 'toys'. Thereafter, Kathleen Kenyon (1967: 101; 1974: 142), in her initial comments on her finds in Jerusalem, which are at the heart of the third lecture, and the authors of numerous popular studies of toys and childhood in Biblical Lands, have cited terracottas as playthings.

Some indeed may well have been toys, either in their primary or secondary use. But, even if their typology does not militate against interpreting them all as toys, their distribution usually does, particularly when the same type is recurrently found in a variety of domestic and cultic contexts, as well as in the graves of adults. Moreover, as Mary Voigt (1983: 188) cogently observed, 'when in use as toys, figurines represent characters or roles in some kind of narrative. The content of this narrative may be related to the ordinary activities of adult men and women in the child's society'.

Indeed, toys provide children with an identity within the world into which they were born, thus relating to it as significantly as do adult images. Any dichotomy between representational objects of recreation and those of symbolic significance for human beings of all ages is not only hard to define for antiquity, but rarely, if ever, likely to be helpful in establishing a basis for the interpretation of such objects. In his renowned statement on the essential role of play in the development of civilization, *Homo Ludens: A Study of the Play-Element in Culture* (1949) Johan Huizinga (1872–1945) has memorably demonstrated that the instinct for play is one of the most fundamental elements of human culture. He concluded that 'the most we can say of the function that is operative in the process of image-making or imagination is that it is a poetic-function; and we define it best of all by calling it a function of play—the *ludic* function, in fact' (Huizinga 1949: 24). That a terracotta might have been a children's toy is arguably the least interesting thing which might be said of it and no justification for then dismissing it out-of-hand as a cultural signifier within the society where it was made. Indeed, it works both ways. There is, for instance, ethnographical evidence for magical figurines recycled as children's playthings (cf. Voigt 2000: 267; Quirke 1998).

The very fact that in the general literature of Biblical Archaeology terracotta images should so readily have been categorized as toys is in itself significant. It indicates the difficulties, in our place and time, of understanding or even sympathetically appraising so alien a cultural phenomenon as that represented by terracotta figurines. An instructive comparison may be made with ancient seals and the surviving clay-sealings impressed with them. They are the primary source of modern information on the iconography of the ancient Near East, not least since stone seals are great survivors.

This has been admirably demonstrated by Othmar Keel and his colleagues in the University of Fribourg, Switzerland, with respect to Canaan, Israel and Judah (Keel and Uehlinger 1998). Obscure as the meaning of ancient glyptic designs and images may sometimes be to the modern observer, their functions are at least generally evident, as indeed are their social contexts. Seals, moreover, still have meaning in our society. Their uses, whether as signatures, talismans or amulets are generally well understood. This may not be said of ancient terracotta figurines, which immediately confront us with various conceptual hazards. Three, in particular, need to be articulated at the outset here:

First, they serviced polytheistic religions, where focus is always diffuse, as it is directed at the many rather than the one. In such religions there is a kaleidoscopic pattern of deities immanent in the physical world that is as far as might be imagined from a religion centred on a single, archetypal 'Mother Goddess', or for that matter 'Father God'. A generation ago, when highlighting the problems presented by polytheism, in a once notorious essay entitled, 'Why a "Mesopotamian Religion" should not be written', the distinguished Assyriologist Leo Oppenheim (1977: 182–183) reached the conclusion that:

> Neither the number of deities worshipped nor the absence or presence of definite (and carefully worded) answers to the eternal and unanswerable questions of man separate decisively a polytheistic from a monotheistic religion. Rather, it seems to be the criterion of plurality of intellectual and spiritual dimensions that sets off most of the higher polytheistic religions from the narrowness, the one-dimensional pressure of revealed religions.

A potential plurality of meanings is accepted here as basic to understanding the role of terracottas in the ancient Near East.

Second, terracotta figurines in the Near East illustrate an intimate relationship of magic and religion in antiquity that is often ignored by the modern tendency to polarize them. 'Magic', Erica Reiner (1995: VIII) has remarked in the light of documentation in Assyro-Babylonian *élite* literature, 'was not a marginal and clandestine manipulation; it was an activity prescribed and overtly practised for the benefit of king and court, or of important individuals—only noxious witchcraft was forbidden and prosecuted'. Although the magic of the common man and woman would appear never to have been written down, even in literate societies, it was no less a potent social force amongst ordinary people, as at times is evident in their material culture. The reason, as Keith Thomas (1997: 668) phrased it in the closing sentence of his definitive study of magic and religion in early modern England, is universal: 'if magic is to be defined as the employment of ineffective techniques to allay anxiety when effective means are not available, then we must recognize that no society will ever be free from it' (cf. Abusch and van der Toorn 1999).

Contemporary anthropologists generally regard any distinction between magic and religion, where both are endemic, as difficult to sustain in their studies of living groups. It is all the more so in retrospective studies of societies where there is little evident sign of magic practices in the archaeological record. Surviving written records from Assyria and Babylonia indicate why this is commonly the case (cf. Reiner 1987; Wiggerman 1986). Even when the materials prescribed for the manufacture of magical figurines were not organic, as they commonly were, the efficacy of the magical prescriptions often depended on the ultimate complete destruction of the images created to promote them.

Recognition of any magical uses in surviving baked clay figurines is notoriously controversial. Many of the terracottas to be discussed in these lectures show signs of breakage. Virtually all were fired as hard as contemporary pottery. As they are recurrently found broken in rubbish, the question of whether or not this was deliberate is endemic in the subject and virtually impossible to resolve categorically in particular cases (cf. Kletter 1996: 54–56, fig. 25). Only when distinct patterns of breakage are evident in closed contexts does the probability gain credence (cf. Franken 1995: 236–237; Nishiyama and Yoshizawa 1997: 83–84); but the possibility should never be entirely ruled out in other cases where the degree of destruction is exceptional.

Third, the terracottas to be discussed here illustrate the manners and customs of communities in which fertility (or maternity) is to be seen as complementary to sexuality not as its polar opposite. If the relationship of magic and religion has to be emancipated from modern western values, so also do many aspects of sexuality and gender (defined as the social aspects of sexuality) in a subject where female images, as often as not naked or partially so, play a central role. As Zainab Bahrani (1996), in particular, has recently argued with respect to Assyro-Babylonian art and literature, traditional western interpretations have too often owed more to the repressions of the Hellenistic and Judeo-Christian traditions than to close study of the primary literary sources where they are available. In ancient Mesopotamian culture chastity and virginity would appear to have had no special importance. Sexuality and fertility (or maternity) were not inextricably linked, with fertility being the excuse for sexuality. Rather they were seen as quite separate and not restricted only to the world of goddesses and women. The sexually active 'Fertility Goddess' of western academic tradition is almost certainly anachronistic when epitomized in such reductionist terms (cf. Westenholz 1998).

Sexuality, as Bahrani argues, in ancient Near Eastern cultures was a metaphor deployed both positively and variously. Images of naked goddesses, distinguished by horned crowns in ancient Mesopotamia, and naked women whose divine or human status is not explicitly stated in a way the modern observer may recognize, had symbolic roles grounded in a lived reality. There women were not expected to maintain a mystique and to conceal their deepest sexual impulses. In Bahrani's analysis various roles in the imagery of the naked female are distinguished: as mother and as sexual partner; as seductress and as entertainer; as goddess and as mortal. Each served a distinct iconographic or literary role, whilst the ideal of female sexuality remained the same.

4. Clay and cuneiform texts: inscribed terracottas in ancient Mesopotamia

A particular strength of Bahrani's exposition is her use of written evidence to supplement her analysis of the visual imagery, whenever possible, as to an unusual degree it is with the texts from ancient Iraq. Certain other aspects of this remarkable legacy are relevant to clay imagery, both anthropomorphic and zoomorphic. Although application of conclusions drawn from it to biblical contexts must always be circumspect, it is more relevant than anything else currently available. The association of clay and the creation of humanity is primeval in the Mesopotamian tradition. There, according to the most common creation myth, mankind was made from clay and 'Potter' was a name of the senior god Enlil (cf. Lambert 1998: 191). In *Genesis* 2: 7–8, when God (Yahweh) forms Adam from earth the Hebrew can also bear the specific meaning 'to pot'. In the Iron Age Levant, as will be investigated in the third lecture, the relative freedom of the potter in the manufacture of terracottas will be contrasted to the very restricted mouldmade repertory of Late Bronze Age Canaan.

In Babylonia, moreover, as Foster (1974) has pointed out, 'the powers of wisemen of old were still accessible and not merely to be found in the continuing process of intellectual achievement or in their literary works that were available to be consulted. These powers were attracted by a simple technique universal in Mesopotamian cult practice: the fashioning of an image and the use of effective language to localize the desired presence in the image'. Yet, even in Mesopotamia, definite instances of the ritual use of figurines in any period remain relatively rare in the current archaeological record. The best documented are the magically protective

Mesopotamia
main sites mentioned in the text

inscribed clay figurines of supernatural beings (deities and demons) recovered by excavation from foundation deposits in Neo-Assyrian public buildings for which complementary ritual texts have also survived in tablet libraries (cf. Green 1983; Wiggerman 1992) (Plate 2).

Somewhat earlier, from the Kassite Period in Babylonia (*c.* 1650–1150 BC), have survived inscribed clay figurines, addressed to the Babylonian deity Gula, the goddess of healing, whose familiar animal was the dog (cf. Black and Green 1992: 101). These are of particular interest here since Nicholas Postgate (1994) has undertaken an instructive analysis of their inscriptions. This bears directly on the possibly distinct roles of anthropomorphic and zoomorphic terracottas elsewhere at this time, not least on contemporary sites in Canaan. These Kassite dedicatory inscriptions reveal a basic dichotomy between human and animal images in the minds of those presenting them.

The clay animals were gifts to the deity (Plate 3); the clay human figurines were suppliants. A sample inscription on an animal terracotta reads thus: 'I brought this effigy to my Lady's (i.e. Gula) attention, may it speak my prayers.' Such clay dogs are always referred to in the inscriptions as 'a dog' not as 'the figurine of a dog' or 'a dog figurine'. In other words, the clay image *is* the thing, representing one of a category, not a specific identity. They were not understood as a channel for communication but rather as substitutes for the real animal.

This was not the case with the inscribed anthropomorphic images. On them, but never on the animals, the Akkadian word for image (*salmum*) is used, whether a natural or a supernatural being is represented. This term refers to a physical representation of another specific identity, not to undifferentiated members of a category. In the light of this terminological distinction Postgate (1994: 179) points out, for instance, that the couples shown on Old Babylonian clay plaques, to be considered here in the second lecture, are to be seen, not as members of a class, but as particular couples. This is one of the very rare cases where a category of these plaques may arguably be related to a category of texts: the so-called potency incantations as, for instance, when one reads, 'you mix together dough (made of) emmer and potter's clay; you make figurines of the man and woman, put them one upon the other and place them at the man's head' (Biggs 1967: 46). The terminology of the correct translation, as here, involves making a figurine of *the* (not *a*) man or woman.

5. Images and imagery: the value of broad and extended perspectives

At each stage in the second and third lectures three questions, (generally unspoken) with regard to the terracottas under discussion, are primary: Who or what is represented? Why are they, or it, being represented? To whom is the image addressed? When anthropomorphic images that lack any specific indication of their natural or supernatural status are under discussion, there is the recurrent danger that the divine audience is being confused with the human suppliant. The 'Judean Pillar Figurines' are a good illustration of this basic dilemma. Is it indeed the goddess Asherah who is represented in human form (or perhaps a famous cult statue of her) or is it a human votary seeking the favours of Asherah, or possibly, of another deity, through the figurine?

Imagery is, of course, not a static phenomenon. It is part of dynamic process of human creativity within specific social contexts. Ernst Gombrich (1993: 75–77) coined the useful phrase 'the ecology of the image' to draw attention to the fact that 'an image may evolve but its ecology, the social context, in its turn reacts back on why images are made, how they are made ... So you may find this very interesting interaction always between the strength of tradition and social *milieu* which allows something to continue'. This is particularly true of societies like those involved in Canaan, Israel and Judah, permeated by religious authority on the one hand, age old folklore and myth on the other. The most striking feature about the manufacture and use of terracottas across the lowland Near East in antiquity is the prevalence of a basic repertory so widely for so long. In such circumstances *la longue durée* schema of Braudel is not only the most appropriate format for seeking to understand their meanings and functions; but also that best calculated to reveal their interactions across the region (cf. Braudel 1980: 25–63).

6. Contrasting terracotta repertories: Canaan, Israel and Judah

It is not always appreciated, since they are often treated separately, how marked was the contrast between the popular terracotta imagery of Canaan in the Late Bronze Age (*c.* 1650–1150 BC), and its legacy, and that of Israel and Judah, particularly the latter, under the Divided Monarchy (*c.* 950–586 BC). At present virtually nothing is known of terracotta imagery in the intervening period of the United Monarchy (cf. Mazar and Camp 2000). The distinctions are both in repertory and in technology.

In Canaan one-piece open-mounds were used to mass produce low relief images of nude females on hand-held clay plaques, arguably used only by women. Only two primary designs are recurrent and widespread in the current archaeological record. Miniature male images at this time were apparently made only of metal in Canaan and deposited in official shrines as terracottas generally were not (Moorey and Fleming 1984). Clay animal figurines were numerous, as they were also to be in Israel and Judah. They are primarily domestic animals, either token sacrificial victims or offerings appropriate to deities regarded as 'mistresses or masters of animals.'

In Israel and Judah not only are the distinctive forms all hand-modelled in the prehistoric manner; but the repertory, with its free-standing male and female images, its animals and models of inanimate objects, recalls that of the early historic period in Iraq and Syria in the third millennium BC, at the time of early state formation there. In Late Bronze Age Canaan production in semi-precious and precious materials of pendants for earrings and necklaces, which replicate the imagery of the clay plaques, suggests that these plaques were *talismans*, magical figurines conceived as benefiting their owners, rather than *icons* themselves regarded as sacred. They represented female personal piety.

The terracottas of Iron Age II in Judah particularly, free-standing and handmodelled, would appear to have been made for rather different circumstances and purposes. This now involved both males who were increasingly portrayed in clay, especially as horse-riders, and females. They imply performance or manipulation, adult game-playing to secure benefits for families or communities, rather than just for individual women, albeit acting as mothers in the best interests of their families. These Iron Age terracottas were encoding hopes and aspirations and mediating social concerns rather different from the Canaanite plaques, even though the intended divine audience might have changed less than was once supposed. The plaques remained current to some extent in Israel, but not in Judah.

7. Some primary considerations

The echoes of prehistory to be found in this Iron Age repertory of terracottas in the Levant extended beyond their free-standing forms, their handmodelling and their comparable range of anthropomorphic, zoomorphic and inanimate subjects. These parallels raise questions about the origins of miniaturization, about the significance of the relatively rare male components of the anthropomorphic repertory and about the interaction of the various terracotta categories, not least in assemblages embodying communal concerns rather than just those of individuals or families.

(a) Why miniaturize?

The pre-pottery Neolithic B village at 'Ain Ghazal (*c.* 8700–7000 BC), in the suburbs of modern Amman in Jordan, on account of the variety of its imagery and matching publications, is the best site in the Levant at present for investigating the origins of miniaturization (cf. Rollefson 2000). The presence there of some of the earliest evidence known for monumental anthropomorphic statuary alongside a wide variety of anthropomorphic and zoomorphic miniature images, handmodelled in clay, allows for instructive comparisons.

It was the custom in this village, as at other contemporary settlements, notably Jericho, to detach the heads from dead bodies of certain adult men and women and then to remodel the features in plaster and clay for display, before eventually burying them in caches in specially cut pits. This practice, to avoid contamination from further use after their involvement in rituals (cf. Garfinkel 1994), will still be central to discussion of controversial archaeological contexts containing terracottas in Iron Age Jerusalem. Whether a private or public practice, this reconstruction of skulls would appear to indicate veneration of certain select members of the community by what memorably, if debatably, Kathleen Kenyon (1956: 186) described as 'the earliest known portraits in the direct line of ancestry of modern art.'

This practice of detaching skulls was widespread in the Levant at this time. Their mobility is significant. First, the actual skulls in Pre-pottery Neolithic A and then those with remodelled features in Pre-Pottery Neolithic B may have represented the transferable aspects of ancestral rights. They were only one aspect of ritual ancestor worship, with the skull representing (*pars pro toto*) a deceased clan or family member. The latter explanation has been extended to embrace some at least of the miniature clay humanoid figurines found at this site, remembering that, as both men and women have female ancestors, the predominance here, as elsewhere throughout prehistory, of female clay figurines need not exclude male concerns.

It is at 'Ain Ghazal, moreover, that plastered skulls were associated with some of the most spectacular examples of anthropomorphic busts and complete statues (between about 35cm. and 90cm. in height), without sexual characteristics, made of painted lime plaster and other materials, which also characterized this period in the Levant. They are made over frameworks of reeds bound with ropes, comparable to the 'straw dollies' of more recent rural communities (cf. Grissom 2000). They were found as caches in pits, like the skulls, apparently carefully buried after use elsewhere.

Some appear to have been already broken when buried, whilst others exhibit clear signs of use, perhaps as the focal points of performances. This hypothesis may be re-inforced by their association at times with anthropomorphic face-masks (cf. Bienert 1990). Both at Jericho and at 'Ain Ghazal some genetic anomalies are depicted in this statuary: feet with six toes and a hand with seven fingers. This is imagery anchored in reality, even if sensitive to anomalies. However, it has been read in two ways, either as depicting human beings, perhaps ancestors or heroes, or supernatural beings. As the case for the existence of an anthropomorphic concept of deity in the Near East remains contentious before the emergence of generally accepted depictions of deities in human form in the earliest Sumerian city-states *c*. 3000 BC, that solution may not be as relevant as it was once commonly assumed to be (cf. *pro*: Cauvin 2000, 105–120; *anti*: Amiet 1995).

Villagers in the Pre-pottery Neolithic Period at 'Ain Ghazal, as elsewhere, also made and used clay miniature images of anthropomorphic and zoomorphic subjects. They were handmodelled, generally unbaked and fragile, and followed closely the simplifications and stylizations of the monumental ones in the case of humanoid forms. At present monumental zoomorphic forms are not evident.

In the transitional stage from hunter-gatherers to the first settled communities, animal figurines had dominated the initial repertories of miniatures. They were to be the most consistent element and commonly the more numerous in any assemblage for millennia, as in Iron Age Jerusalem. At 'Ain Ghazal, moreover, there is to be observed at the outset a persistent trend in favour of conventional forms. Their makers were not, in the majority of cases, seeking to reproduce the natural shapes of bovids, goat and sheep, rather to exploit their natural forms for symbolic purposes. Indeed, it is possible, particularly with those not baked before deposition (cf. McAdam 1997: 135), that they underwent a series of performative mutations in the course of their use. Zoomorphic forms at times appear to merge into anthropomorphic ones, making clear distinctions impossible to the modern eye; but arguably redundant.

At 'Ain Ghazal anthropomorphic terracotta figurines were never found with their heads attached, only as headless bodies or bodyless heads, reflecting the burial practices of the community. This decapitation of images may already be a deliberate attempt to kill their potency. More significantly they were disposed of like routine domestic rubbish, not carefully placed in special pits as was the larger plaster statuary. This distinguishes from the outset potentially different roles for the monumental and the miniature, enigmatic as they may be in retrospect.

Franken (1995: 237), with reference to the Iron Age figurines of Jerusalem, to which we shall return in the third lecture, isolates clay miniatures as 'fetishes', which he defines as instruments of magic, 'made or required *ad hoc*, to be discarded when the occasion no longer requires them'. By contrast, an image (say of the Virgin and Child) is a 'deliberate repetition which can occur again and again, ever anew . . . perpetuation and confirmation of historical fact: what was, is also present here and now.'

The miniatures of 'Ain Ghazal may already represent the rituals of households rather than those of the village as a community. Ellen McAdam (1997, 136), in publishing them, has pointed out that '53 figurines from 20 contexts occurred in groups of 2 or more, and 31 from 9 contexts in groups of 3 or more, suggesting that many of them derived from "discrete episodes of activity"' (cf. Schmandt-Besserat 1977: 52, fig.13). The extreme fragility of unbaked figurines, which constituted the majority here, and the damage they suffered as they dried out after excavation, certainly does not suggest extended use. As many were found here, as elsewhere, mixed in with ash amongst household debris, baking may always have been a chance consequence of disposal practices at this time.

Their small scale allowed terracottas to be taken in hand; the unbaked medium allowed them to be easily modified. Whatever they encoded might through them be defined and controlled in episodes, after which, it would appear, they were regarded as disposable with household rubbish. They were not thought, unlike the more monumental images, to require special treatment. In general, their use remains obscure; another persistent characteristic. There is, however, at least one case of what Ucko and Voigt would term 'vehicles of magic' characterized by cheap materials, simple forms, and brief episodes of use with careful rather than casual disposal perhaps reflecting the potency of such ritual. Two clay figurines of quadrupeds were found placed in a pit below a lime-plaster floor. One had been pierced three times with flint blades before firing and the head of the other stabbed twice.

Levi-Strauss (1966, 23–4) has defined the role of miniature modelling as primarily a means of achieving authority over the animate or inanimate subjects modelled, as in the performance of magic. The transfer of miniature images from myth-making into ritual enactments, what I shall call here their performative potential, created amongst these pioneers of settled life in agricultural communities a feeling of control over the hazards and vicissitudes of their daily lives in general. With time the frequent, and enduring, miniaturization of the human, the animal and, much more rarely, such inanimate forms as buildings, furniture and vehicles, may be set with more confidence into specific socio-political contexts. Yet throughout specific explanations almost always remain elusive.

(b) Male terracottas: when and why?

A case in point very relevant to the repertory of terracottas in Iron Age Judah and Israel is the sporadic rather than the regular appearance of male anthropomorphic figurines. It is a commonplace of ancient Near Eastern terracotta studies that specifically female images consistently predominated over male in the anthropomorphic range, especially in prehistory. However, it has only recently become more evident that their general rarity until late in prehistory may be explained in part by their use in 'male spaces' separate from domestic contexts within villages. In the Pre-pottery Neolithic B site of Nevali Çorî (*c.* 8000 BC), in a small valley in the Taurus foothills near the Euphrates, distinguished by remarkable monumental stone sculptures (cf. Cauvin 2000, pl.III: 6), the terracotta figurine count was recently reported as : 22.5% female, 26.7% male; 5.8% non sex-specific humanoid; 4.4% zoomorphic; and 40% unclassified fragments in a total of 670 recovered (Morsch 1998). Whether this is a special case remains to be seen.

It is not, however, until four thousand years later on present evidence that explicitly male figurines become a recurrent, if still minor, constituent of terracotta repertories in southern Iraq, amongst the steadily more socially complex settlements of the so-called Samarra and Ubaid cultures. Here by the fifth and into the fourth millennium BC there are increasing signs of a standardisation and professional production of terracottas now intimately associated by their painted decoration with contemporary pottery. They are the first clear indication of such imagery used to demonstrate and re-enforce changing human social roles through the most popular form of three-dimensional representation. The traditional sitting or squatting pose of females is now replaced by standing or reclining forms for both sexes, whilst the differences between their body forms are minimized in similar overall proportions, with broad shoulders and tapering hips. Cranial deformation, masklike features, and androgynous body ornamentation for both sexes suggest *élite* or specialist social groups defining and encoding their status, as do representations of males in litters or wearing what may be crested helmets (Ellen McAdam: personal communication; cf. Wengrow 1998).

The culmination of these trends in Sumer in the early third millennium was a major change in the repertory of humanoid terracottas. For the first time females passed into eclipse and males emerged as a distinct element, sometimes in close association with models of wheeled vehicles and traction animals. Such miniatures reflect the emergence in the real world of new male *élites* in the pristine city-states of the region (cf. Watelin 1934: pl.XIV; Woolley 1955: pl.24). As anthropologists (cf. Rapp 1977) have pointed out, the forces of early state formation in general maginalize female roles so, in this, Sumer was no exception. Indeed in a recent reconstruction of the evolution of the Sumerian divine pantheon, Steinkeller (1999, 113–14) speculated that its growing masculisation at this time also reflected major structural changes in Sumerian society.

This is a particularly clear case of terracottas encoding and mediating socio-political change. The new Sumerian male *élite* used these ephemeral popular objects, amongst other symbols, to establish and sustain their position in a generally illiterate society, in ways later more readily associated with writing and public art and, in our time, with the mass media. Significantly, another main concern of new ruling groups, the sanctification of their power by religious endorsement of its legitimacy, is evident at this time on *élite* objects with restricted circulation. They illustrate the manipulation of symbols to negotiate social and political prestige in seal designs and in sculptured reliefs, both fixed to walls and carved on stone bowls.

The crudely handmade clay images appear to be ephemeral objects, often so schematic as to be barely recognizable, like many of their prehistoric ancestors. It is as if they had been given an identity for an occasion and no less swiftly annihilated thereafter. They are best known from deposits of very miscellaneous urban rubbish in Iraq in Early Dynastic I-II (*c.* 3000–2750 BC) at sites like Kish and Ur (cf. Moorey 1978, 99–103; McAdam 1993, 88–9) and in Early Dynastic III (*c.* 2750–2350 BC) at Abu Salabikh (cf. McAdam 1993), where they are associated in a rubbish deposit with clay tokens, miniature vessels, clay sealings and cuneiform tablet fragments. Save for the tablet fragments, this assemblage is powerfully reminiscent of the precocious bureaucratic practices already evident in the sixth millennium BC, as 'archives before writing', at Tell Sabi Abyad in Syria. But there, the anthropomorphic terracottas were all female and headless (cf. Akkermans and Verhoeven 1995: 25–6, fig. 15).

PLATE 1

Handmade seated female terracotta with painted details (the so-called 'Mother Goddess' type); excavated at Chagar Bazar, Syria; Halaf Period, *c.* 5500–5000 BC; 10 cm high. (1936.90).

PLATE 2

Inscribed handmade terracotta guardian dog; excavated at Kish in Iraq; seventh to sixth century BC; 6.7 cm high. (1924.302).

PLATE 3

Inscribed handmade terracotta 'bitch' (as inscription); excavated at Kish in Iraq; c. 2000 BC; 5 cm long (1931.67).

PLATE 4

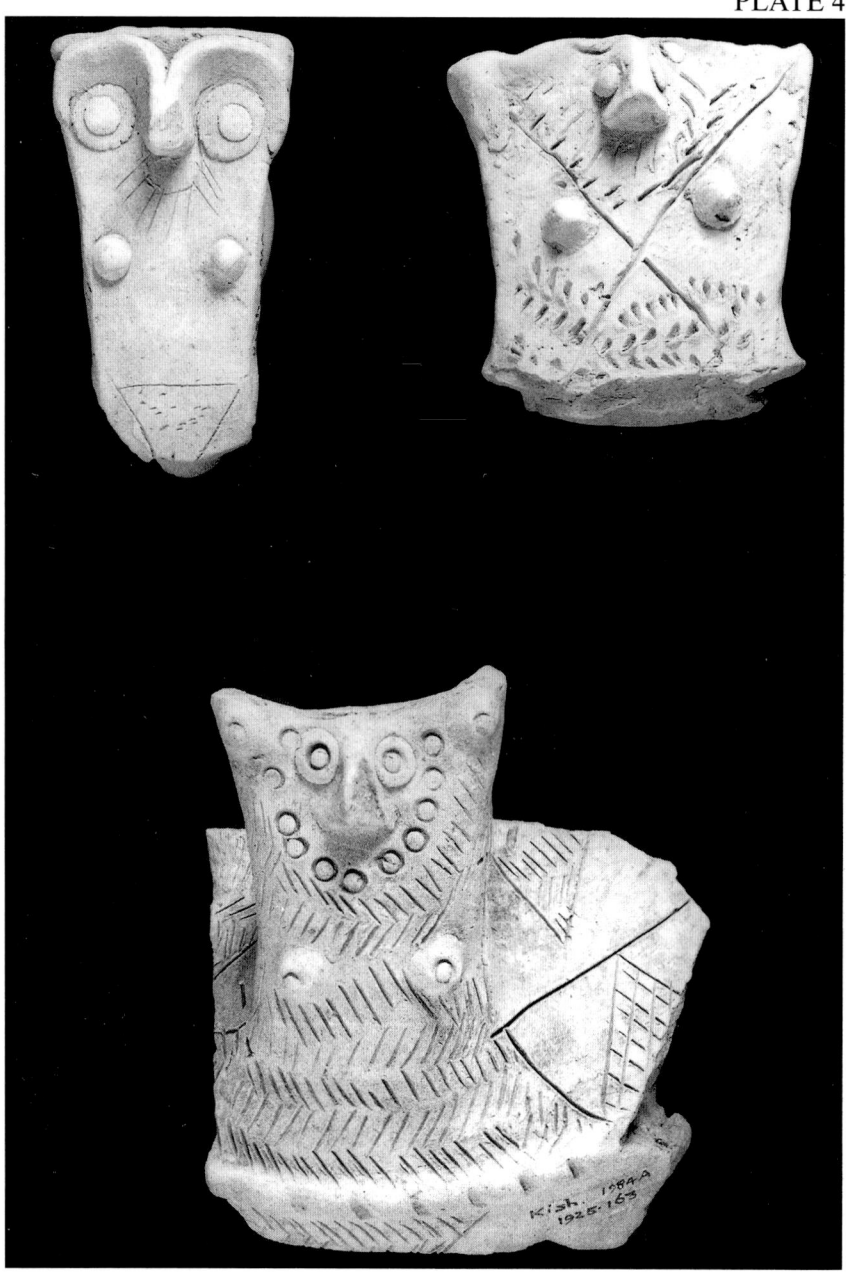

Handmade 'Mother Goddess handles' from pottery storage jars; excavated at Kish ('Cemetery A') in Iraq; *c.* 2500 BC; 8 cm, 8 cm, 7.6 cm high (1925.163, 166, 167).

These free-standing, handmodelled terracottas were an integral part of the process of regulating access to literacy and associated social roles in one of the earliest state systems known to us. Here, as two thousand years later, when such handmodelled male and female terracottas appear again, this time in Israel and Judah, the activities or performances in which they played a part, may only be guessed at. On the face of it, in both cases, their overall social context is primary, with any religious aspect, however important, only a part of it. In prehistoric and early historic contexts the shaping of these objects might in some way have been part of the procedures at male-dominated occasions, like banquets, where exchange and ritual were primary concerns (cf. McAdam 1993). Again later, in the Iron Age in Israel and Judah, male terracottas indicate changes in the social order in ways that are not usually evident with the females.

(c) Conceiving terracottas as units of varied types rather than just as single types

Both in Prehistory and in the Iron Age terracottas survive as single pieces not as units. They are like chessmen scattered randomly without either surviving boards to give them coherent relationships or guidelines for acting them out in ritualized play. An extremely rare model in clay allows for a brief glimpse of a terracotta community embracing all the primary types, anthropomorphic, zoomorphic and inanimate recurrent in these lectures. That it should be Cypriot is not surprising. The richness and variety of clay modelling found on Cyprus in antiquity in imitation of the real rather than the mythical world is marked. This is neatly reflected in a tale related in the twelfth century A.D. by the scholar Eustathius, when commenting on a passage in Homer's *Iliad* (II: 20), ' [Kinyras] had sworn in Paphos to despatch fifty ships to Menelaos, but sent only one. The rest he made out of clay, placing clay-men in them. These he sent, thus evading his oath by paying honour with a terracotta army' (cf. Reyes 1994: 22).

In 1931, in the course of excavating the late third millennium BC tomb no. 22 at Bellapais-Vounous, on the northern coast of Cyprus, Dikaios (1938) found a clay model of a circular enclosure populated with figurines. It has a single entrance. It contains nineteen anthropomorphic images and two pairs of bovids in pens. Immediately across from the entrance on the opposite wall is a series of horizontal and vertical pilasters crowned at the top by bull-heads. The area in front of them is set-off from the rest by a low floor-ridge. These images are flanked by benches against the wall accommodating seated men; in front of them an enthroned male, his larger scale emphasizing exceptional status, wears a distinctive headdress. To the right of him stand six males in a circle looking inwards. On the left closest to the entrance a standing woman, holding a child, looks into the bovid pen, accompanied by two standing males. Two more males stand close to the right-hand bovid pen. All the males in the enclosure have their arms folded.

This tomb-model has usually been interpreted on the understanding that funerary equipment has significance both for the living and the dead and that, with whatever intent, it portrays a ceremony focused on the wall symbols. Diversity of interpretation enters in with attempts to treat it, on the one hand, simply as a scene from everyday life, as are found on contemporary pottery (cf. Morris 1985: 283–4), or on the other to postulate specific religious or sociological explanations for the whole or parts of it (cf. Peltenburg 1994). It is significant that each interpreter tends to give only one interpretation. Current trends in prehistoric terracotta studies, however, emphasize the need for an awareness of the potential ambiguities in such popular imagery and the value of not privileging one interpretation over another, so long as each is well grounded in the available evidence. 'The interpretation of figurines should be presented *in relation to*, not in exclusion of, alternative interpretative narratives' is how Tringham and Conkey (1998: 45) recently put it.

Ancient Near Eastern terracottas were as much artefacts as were the everyday pots often made, used and disposed of with them. By their actions people incorporated them into their perceptions and value systems and necessarily embedded them in their social settings. But anything that lives changes. Objects like chameleons change their meanings (or rather have their meanings changed) as they are successively embedded in different settings. That is what makes investigating them so fascinating, yet so hazardous if over simplified, as it will be my purpose to demonstrate in the next two lectures in relation first to Bronze Age Canaan, then to Iron Age Israel and Judah.

II

Terracottas in Early Complex Societies: Sumer, Babylonia, Syria, Egypt and Canaan (*c*. 3000–1150 BC)

1. Contrasts in the terracotta imagery of Canaan, Israel and Judah

The extended timescale embraced in this lecture, some two thousand, five hundred years, and the equally wide geographical range, from Egypt to Iraq through the Levant, needs justification at the outset. Such a vast canvas is compensated for by the narrowness of the theme and the constancy of the medium through which it was carried across time and space. The theme is epitomized by a youthful, nude female shown full-frontal in low relief, with and without attributes, on hand held clay plaques, which were mass-produced to relatively standard patterns in one-piece open moulds. Her identity in most times and places, as with so many of the female images to be discussed in these lectures, is notoriously enigmatic. In almost every context where they appear their functions are no less obscure. Yet they epitomize popular Canaanite imagery in clay, not only in the Late Bronze Age (*c*. 1650–1150 BC), when Canaan was part of the Egyptian Empire, but thereafter as part of the Canaanite legacy to the new states of the southern Levant.

These plaques offer rare access to the popular rituals of women, as distinct from those of male-dominated official, temple-based cults in Late Bronze Age Canaan. This was the image, in particular, that was rejected by the people of Judah, and to a less extent those of Israel, when, under the Divided Monarchy, terracottas reverted to the hand-modelling techniques and the varied anthropomorphic, zoomorphic and inanimate miniatures familiar in prehistory. They will be the subject of the third lecture.

It was only towards the end of the last century that it was increasingly acknowledged amongst Old Testament scholars that evidence for an early Israelite popular cult of goddesses was strong. Indeed, van der Toorn (1998: 96) recently pointed out that in the daily devotions of ordinary

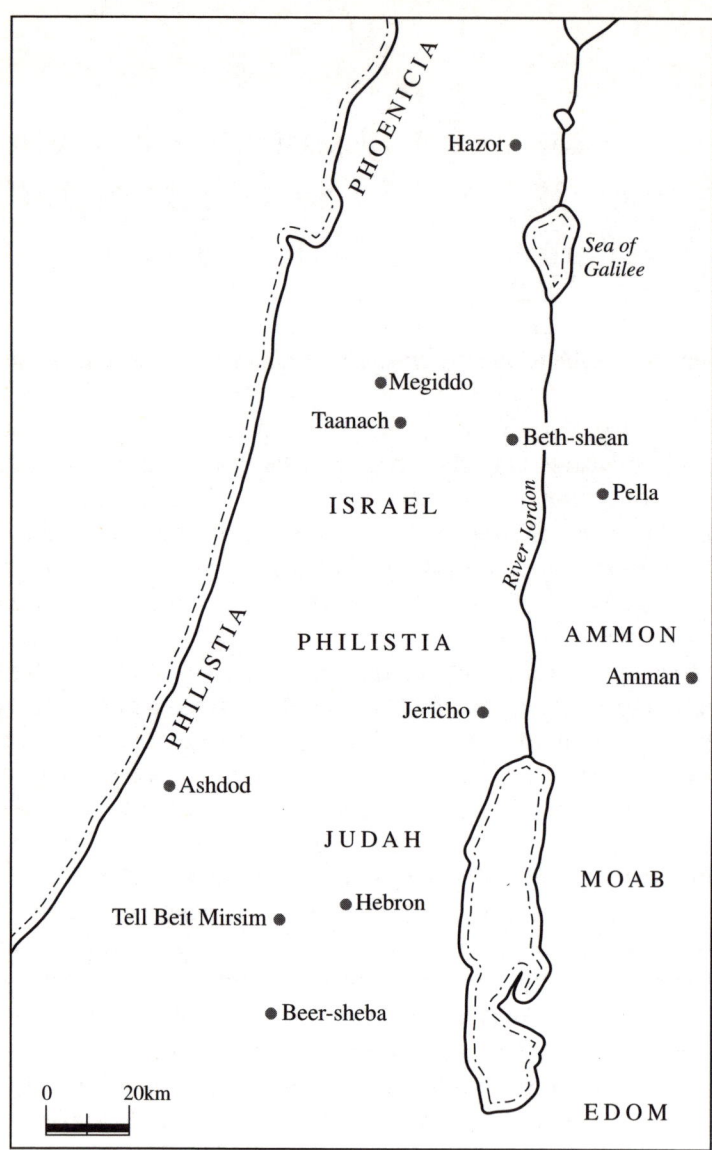

Map of sites in the Bronze and Iron Age Levant
(Canaan occupied most of the area west of the Jordan)

people: 'goddesses seem to have played a role inversely proportional to their official importance.' This lecture will examine the Canaanite background to this phenomenon as evident in terracotta imagery in the Late Bronze Age, before the emergence of the people of Israel, and thereafter when it was rejected in Judah and minimally evident in Israel, although it survived until the Achaemenid Persian Empire in Syria and elsewhere in the Near East and Cyprus.

Canaan is defined for present purposes as the area south of the modern Lebanon, west of the river Jordan, to the frontier with Egypt, her imperial overlord in the period in question, *c.* 1650–1150 BC, archaeologically the Late Bronze Age. Egypt's cultural impact was considerable; but Canaan's traditional religion owed much to a Syro-Mesopotamian heritage, as did many elements in her art. Any study of her popular imagery must then take account of the potential impact both of her northern and of her southern neighbour. Fortunately, they had very distinctive characteristics of their own, reflected in their religious iconography. These influences will be examined here in turn, in so far as they bear on the genesis of the common nude female images of Canaan.

2. **The emergence of nude female images in early urban societies in Sumer (*c.* 3000–2100 BC)**

At the end of the first lecture it was noted how the female terracotta images, so characteristic of the village settlements in the prehistoric Near East, were eclipsed at the time of early state formation in southern Iraq (ancient Sumer) in the centuries on either side of 3000 BC. The new controlling male *élites* then used terracottas, with male images and chariots most conspicuous amongst them, in ways subsequently more readily associated with writing, to encode and define their authority and status. When female images are encountered during excavations in these pristine city-states in Sumer, they are not the variously modelled statuettes in painted pottery familiar in Sumer in the Samarra and Ubaid cultures of later prehistory.

They are now flat, stylized nude silhouettes of the female body with eyes, but no mouth (as in prehistory). Sexual characteristics were depicted. Already, as was to become common, particular attention was at times paid to elaborate hair-styling and jewellery. These figurines fit very comfortably into the palm of the hand, as if to grasp them was at least part of the intention. They come from domestic contexts, not from deposits in the shrines of the now state-controlled temples. They have, consequently, been identified as talismans, perhaps grasped during childbirth, or at other times of crisis and stress, by women in their private lives. Mortuary deposit appears to have been exceptional rather than routine (cf. Dales 1960: nos. 72–9; Frankfort 1936, fig. 57). The identity of the image is unknown.

It is in the middle of the third millennium BC, as an aspect of pottery production, that a highly stylized female image first appears in Sumer which anticipates the nude females of the following centuries. These crude, handmodelled devices, without any trace of horned headdresses or other signifiers of divinity, appear as the upright handles of storage jars in various sizes, including miniatures, manufactured in central and southern Iraq. What the jars contained is unknown, though dry goods, perhaps grain, appear more probable than liquids, for which spouted jars were provided. There is a whole series of these handles from plain or simply incised to elaborate, at times almost grotesque, nude female images, with their jewellery, breasts and genitals emphasized (cf. Moon 1987) (Plate 4).

One of their most instructive appearances is in the graves of Cemetery A at Kish, east of the site of Babylon. Here the burial area, overlying an earlier royal palace, was adjacent to a major temple complex dedicated to the goddess Inanna-Ishtar. (cf. Moorey 1978: 67–8). In her primeval form at Uruk, the oldest known Sumerian town, she was the spirit or presiding deity of the community's central storehouse. Subsequently, she was to remain the most important goddess in the Sumero-Babylonian pantheon, with a multiplicity of aspects embracing at least three major characteristics: in astral contexts, as the planet Venus, the morning and evening star; in war and combat; and in love and sexual behaviour (cf. Black and Green 1992: 108–9; Westenholz 1998: 72–4).

She was not, however, a goddess of marriage or a mother goddess, despite the fact that jars like those from Kish have been popularly known as 'Mother Goddess Jars' for the better part of a century. In a famous hoard of contemporary precious objects from Mari in modern Syria, (but culturally then part of ancient Sumer) nude female statuettes in ivory, metal and bone, are shown both with and without horns. This already complicates any attempt to define their status (cf. Parrot 1968) simplistically as supernatural or natural (human) images. The anthropomorphic jar handles, without horns, have been regarded as representing acolytes of the Goddess, perhaps shown ritually nude in her presence, as male caryatids on metal temple offering-stands certainly were at this time. The horned crown was already, as later, in Babylonia the primary indication of divine status.

Goddesses were no less various in character than gods in the ancient Near East. Moreover, men as well as women petitioned goddesses about problems in their personal lives. These anthropomorphic jar-handles reflect in explicit terms for the first time in the archaeological record what has every appearance of being a controlled iconography manipulated by state religious authorities through temple potteries. Later, once standardized moulded clay plaques were widely circulated, it is extremely rare for the centres of generation and distribution to be known. Here the work of craft-potters is evident, providing standardized mortuary equipment in various patterns and sizes. In so far as the inadequate skeletal records for cemetery A allow for conclusions it would appear that these jars were placed both in male and female graves (cf. Moorey 1970).

By now crude handmade free-standing miniature clay images of males and females, shown as offering-bearers or worshippers, were current. A unique handle, more recent than those found at Kish, excavated by Woolley (1934: pl.187a) detached from its jar in the area of the 'Royal Cemetery' at Ur, shows a dressed female with one arm down her side, the other bent at the elbow and held across the chest. This maybe dated in the Akkadian Dynasty (*c*. 2350–2150 BC) and exactly parallels a common type of free-standing female votive figurine much in evidence elsewhere at this time (Plate 5).

This is the first appearance of the columnar body-form, representing ankle-length male and female garments, which allowed them to stand upright on a suitable surface. This is the 'pillar-shape' of which much has been made in Judean Iron Age contexts, where it has been seen as reflecting the tree-like form of the symbol of the Canaanite goddess Asherah, when female terracottas are made this way. It is only necessary at this stage to make the point that this does not sufficiently take into account its previous role over many centuries, in both monumental and minor art, as the standard form for the lower body of upright figures, being not only elegant, stable and simple to make, but also a direct reflection of real costumes. Like their prehistoric ancestors these figurines have pinched features, omitting the mouth. They represent human suppliants; none wears the horned crown by now standard for divinities. Some bear offerings in their hands.

It was towards the end of the Akkadian Period (*c*. 2200 BC) that the most significant single innovation in the technology of terracotta production, before the first millennium BC, was made in Babylonia. Recently

Elise Auerbach (1994: 74–6) established that the earliest well-dated relief clay plaques made in one-piece open moulds were found seventy years ago in the Diyala Valley, east of Baghdad, in levels transitional between the Akkadian and Ur III dynasties at the end of the third millennium BC. From the outset, it would appear that these mass-produced, relatively stereotyped hand-held moulded images were not made for use specifically in religious buildings, even though it has been assumed their production was controlled by the religious authorities. They did not immediately supersede the production of free-standing handmade zoomorphic or anthropomorphic images.

It is probably not a coincidence that it was under the Akkadian kings Naram-Sin (*c.* 2254–2218 BC) and Shar-kali-sharri (*c.* 2217–2193 BC) that handled brick-stamps were introduced to facilitate mass-production of standard royal brick inscriptions in finely cut cuneiform letters (cf. Driver 1948, pl.19). They, like the moulds, illustrate an official concern at the highest level with promulgating approved signs and images as effectively as might be.

The appearance of the one-piece open mould for clay plaque manufacture heralded two or three centuries of production uniquely diversified in the range of images produced in Babylonia. This innovation broadly coincided with an evident standardization in the designs of Babylonian cylinder seals, for which indeed it has been suggested 'pattern books' of some kind may have existed (cf. Collon 1986: 4). There was yet another act of codification at this time, the writing down of Sumerian literature. This may perhaps be explained by the contemporary passing of Sumerian as a living language (cf. van de Mieroop 1997: 223). Diverse as these phenomena are, they all seem to illustrate a concern for intellectual and ideological co-ordination, both within the ruling *élite* and beyond, at least in the urban population. As archaeology reveals nothing yet of village life at this time, terracottas may only be studied as an urban phenomenon.

3. The 'Nude Female' in Babylonia, *c.* 2000–1650 BC

The Babylonian ancestry of the Canaanite clay relief plaques illustrating nude females has been less explored than their more immediate Egyptian antecedents, to be considered later (cf. Keel and Uehlinger 1998: 7–97); but it is no less illuminating. No word in Akkadian or Sumerian has yet been identified for the mouldmade plaques of Babylonia and no certainly genuine example of this period has yet been published from the region with a cuneiform inscription incised into it before baking or scratched on it afterwards. Their function is enigmatic; the more so in view of their diversity. They embrace 'snapshots' or frozen glimpses of many themes: individual deities or demons with distinctive iconography; what may be scenes from myths and legends; vignettes of men, women and animals in their ordinary lives that are at times surprisingly realistic and vivid (cf. Opificius 1961). This striking combination of the natural and the supernatural, of what in modern western eyes might be 'the acceptable' and 'the unacceptable' or the 'proper' and the 'improper', epitomizes my concern in the first lecture with articulating various cultural filters so often set between us and them. In assessing this imagery any facile distinctions between the religious and the secular, magic and religion, sexuality and maternity, have to be dismissed. They are too often symbiotic in these images.

A recurrent theme in any discussion of terracottas, that will be particularly significant in the third lecture with respect to Iron Age Judean examples, is the question of deliberate breakage to destroy the magical power with which a plaque or three-dimensional image might have been ritually endowed. Although in Mesopotamia plaques are reported from time to time that have obviously been repaired with bitumen in antiquity, this seems to have been much more the exception than the rule. Commonly, they are recovered there both battered and broken, as well as complete, in a variety of contexts. They are common within buildings, courtyards, open spaces and streets.

For example, in House J (Area TB) at Nippur, the 'Holy City' of Babylonia, which had served both as a private residence and a public building associated with the administration of agriculture, the excavator reported that: 'the large number of clay figurines (hand-made and mould-made males, nude females, animals and anthropomorphic rattles), mould-made plaques (including plaques with a presentation scene, a bull-man, Gilgamesh slaying Humbaba and a Humbaba head), model chairs and beds with moulded decoration, and model boats are both interesting and problematic. These artefacts were scattered throughout the building, but roughly half were in the courtyards' (Zettler 1996: 92). They appear to be virtually absent from graves (cf. Pruss and Novak 2000) throughout Babylonia.

At Ur, excavated by Woolley, within the city walls terracottas were found in similar contexts, but also associated both with small community shrines set at street corners and with domestic altars, sometimes above vaulted tombs in houses (cf. Woolley and Mallowan 1976: 171–82, pl.66–91; Brusasco 1999–2000: 72). Many, however, were also found on the surface of an extra-mural area which Woolley identified as an industrial suburb, where terracottas, amongst other things, had been made. Regrettably contextual information of this kind is still all too rare in excavation reports on Canaanite towns.

Two sets of these Babylonian terracotta plaques introduce basic questions equally relevant to their Canaanite counterparts: *first*, when a deity is represented, clearly defined in Babylonia by the horned crown, was the deity *per se* intended or only a well-known cult-image of the god or goddess in question? *Second*, who is the nude female, without a horned crown, whose counterpart in Canaan virtually monopolizes the Canaanite repertory of mouldmade anthropomorphic images?

In an essay on Mesopotamian religion, cited in the first lecture, Leo Oppenheim (1977: 184) made a particular point of emphasizing that: 'the role of the image was central in the cult as well as in private worship, as the wide distribution of cheap replicas of such images [in clay] shows' (Plate 6). In Babylonia there is evidence to suggest that commonly, if not invariably, it was indeed a cult statue that was illustrated. Plaques showing a bull-eared god, whose horned crown is depicted from the front, as if it belonged to a fore-shortened and abbreviated rendering of a three-dimensional statue, has been cited as a case in point (cf. Woolley and Mallowan 1976: pl.75: 102). Some of the images of goddesses that were widely distributed in Babylonia have the appearance of sculpted busts or enthroned statues, richly dressed and bejewelled as were the actual cult images within their shrines ('houses').

Such major cult images in Babylonia and Canaan, as is clear from the denunciations of them by Old Testament prophets (cf. *Isaiah* 44: 12–20), were conceived as much more than man-made effigies (cf. Walker and Dick 1999). The major images were prepared from wood and precious materials on a large scale, in accord with elaborate prescriptions intended to transform the lifeless materials into a living incarnation of the deity. This presence was maintained thereafter through daily ceremonials at the heart of a temple. Equally, as and when required, it was ritually removed. A monument in the British Museum, with associated inscription, illustrates the relationship of cult images and clay replicas of them particularly well.

In 1881 Rassam, when excavating at Sippar in Iraq, found a stone tablet (cf. Collon 1995: pl.135; 29.5 cm. high), on which is carved in low relief a depiction of the cult-image of the sun-god Shamash, the city-god, in his primary shrine. This, in itself, is a very rare and vivid glimpse into a Babylonian 'holy of holies'. For present purposes the accompanying text is more significant. It is dated to the thirty-first year of Nabu-apla-iddina, King of Babylon (c. 887–855 BC), a contemporary of the more famous Assyrian king Assur-nasir-pal II (883–859 BC). It records that two hundred years earlier, the Sutians had destroyed the cult-image of Shamash in a raid on Sippar. In the intervening years a sun-disk had been used as a symbolic equivalent. But now, at last, the original had been (divinely) revealed, as the inscription records: 'a relief of his (i.e. Shamash) image, an impression of baked clay of his figure and his insignia, on the opposite bank of the Euphrates on the west bank was discovered' (Walker and Dick 1999: 59–63; col.III: lines 19 ff.). This did not, of course, share the divine presence of the original lost image.

The local priest showed this to the King, who commanded him to have the monumental image remade. This case illustrates how the god and his cult-image were regarded as one, so that when the image was lost so was Shamash. The clay relief alone made possible the manufacture of a new cult-image. That this may well have involved a pious fraud at the time, does not detract from the value of this case as an illustration of the relationship of cult-image and clay replica or copy. Some Egyptologists (cf. Schulman 1981) believe that representations of deities in New Kingdom Egypt, at the time when she ruled Canaan, show a renowned cult statue rather than the deity *per se*. It is then possible, that the two most powerful foreign influences on Canaanite clay imagery shared this convention, even if it remains difficult to identify with certainty in particular cases.

The motif in the Babylonian terracotta tradition most relevant to Canaan, the nude female, is shown without horned headdress and always full frontal (*en face*) (Plate 7). She is of fundamental importance to this inquiry. I use the term 'Nude Female' without prejudice in any circumstance to her status, whether natural or supernatural. In Canaan she monopolized the terracotta repertory, whilst in Babylonia, although one motif amongst many, she is, in variant forms, the most commonly encountered terracotta image on most archaeological sites of the earlier second millennium BC, sometimes in assemblages, sometimes as scattered individuals. She is difficult both to categorize simply or to place in context convincingly. When shown in frieze on cylinder seals with other figures her image is almost defiantly isolated or self-contained.

On cylinder seals, which provide the essential source of comparative information in this case, her frontality particularly distinguishes her in the friezes produced by rolling such seals. Virtually all other figures are shown in profile. It may be significant, recalling that such seals were amulets as well as marks of identity, that she is often placed adjacent to well-documented apotropaic symbols, including those especially associated with fertility, such as bulls and scorpions. At times, both on clay plaques and seals (cf. Black and Green 1992, fig. 118), she is shown standing on a plinth or podium, as if representing a statue. On seals such evident mortals as kings and priests are also sometimes elevated in this way, but presented in profile unlike her (cf. Collon 1986, pl. XXII–III). This would appear to place the nude female in a special category, yet amongst the mortals rather than the immortals as if she was a mediating figure or beneficent spirit that was betwixt and between. Both on seals and plaques she is at times accompanied by dancers and musicians (cf. Collon 1986, nos. 289–90). This is an association found also in Canaanite cities and their successors, where music and dancing were an aspect of rituals, as they had been since prehistory. The nude female in Babylonia appears on seals inscribed both for women and men.

One monumental Mesopotamian stone image, now in the British Museum, found in a ditch near the Temple of Ishtar at Nineveh, may assist with defining the character and function of this image, though it is more recent in date and from an Assyrian context. This nude female (Collon 1995, pl.94; 94 cm. high), having lost her head and forearms, presents an initial problem in that it may not consequently be said whether or not she originally wore a horned crown. However, she is inscribed on the back, in the name of Ashur-bel-kala, King of Assyria (*c.* 1073–1056 BC), as follows (in Grayson's (1991: 108) translation): 'I made these sculptures in the provinces, cities and garrisons for titillation (in the sense of sexual allure); for the one who removes my inscriptions and my name: the divine Sibitti, the gods of the west, will afflict him with snake-bite.' The fact that these statues had been mass-produced, as well as the tone of the text, suggest she is mortal and probably to be identified as an acolyte or servant of the Goddess Ishtar.

Zainab Bahrani (1996: 12, nn.55–6), who recently made a special study of female imagery in Mesopotamia, has proposed that the carefully depicted young woman's breasts and genital curls graphically endorse the intention of the royal inscription. One of Ishtar's many roles was as the youthful goddess of love (cf. Westenholz 1998: 73). Bahrani fortifies her argument with citations from Babylonian literature in which she believes that the female body was identified with nubility and sexuality rather than with fertility. She adduces in support of her case those clay plaques explicitly depicting sexual intercourse and also those examples where it is implied for a nude female reclining on a bed (Plate 8), one hand on her abdomen, the other raised at the side of her head or where she is accompanied by a disembodied phallus (cf. de Meyer 1978: pl.27: 6). It is part of Bahrani's case that in the Babylonian world maternity and sexuality were regarded as complementary not, as in the modern western world, as polar opposites.

Wiggermann (1985–6: 28–9; 1998: 52–3), who has been responsible recently for the most intensive examination and assessment of the documentary evidence for the status and role of the Babylonian nude female, does not find any evidence to sustain a case for regarding her as a goddess. He defines her status in light of the Akkadian word *baštu*, from a verb meaning 'to be ashamed; to disgrace (with sexual connotations)' (cf. *Chicago Assyrian Dictionary*: **B**: 142–4). Thus she is to be characterized as a protective spirit personifying female dignity or, put another way, as guarantor of personal happiness. The sexual connotation of her status is materially endorsed by the existence of an inscribed bronze votive-offering in the shape of a female genitals, excavated at Assur in Assyria, on which the object is described as *baštu* (cf. Jacob-Rost and Freydank 1981). In the light of this interpretation Wiggermann (1998: 52–3) conceives this image as embodying various sexual emotions and good luck. Amongst Babylonian goddesses he associates her particularly with Inanna (Ishtar). Thus, though he did not make the connection, recalling the much earlier nude females shown on the jar handles from Cemetery A at Kish, which lay alongside a major temple of this goddess, as described at the beginning of this lecture.

In the ancient Near East deities represented certain functions and their help was sought in specific circumstances. In Babylonia, and almost certainly elsewhere, goddesses of healing or private life might be petitioned either by men or women, directly or indirectly. This image, at least for women, would appear to have been a vital intermediary in diverse cultural settings but not as a ranking deity, rather as a spirit who was regarded by a human petitioner as a 'propitious being', acceptable to the goddess as an emissary for humanity. The contrast may be made precisely by comparing her with those images in Babylonian art of a standing *en face* nude female who does wear the horned crown and often has the characteristics of a bird (wings and claws). It has been demonstrated that she belongs with the creatures of the underworld (cf. Black and Green 1992: 144; Jacobsen 1987).

In a richly illustrated major monograph published twenty years ago Urs Winter (1983) provided a fully documented account of the Nude

Female, with an explanation of her function that has been influential in Old Testament Studies. For him she was a goddess whose identity had varied with cultural context. His all embracing interpretation of her role turns on the idea that individual women identified with the goddess, whoever she might have been in a particular context. Through the image moulded on a handheld clay plaque each woman conceived of her as an exemplary woman. If this could be demonstrated it would render superfluous questions about the divine or mortal status of the female depicted. Then, in the words of Keel and Uehlinger (1998: 108): 'the plaques would portray the goddess *as* a woman, and conversely they identify the female worshipers [using] the plaques with the goddess.' However, in the absence of any unequivocal literary evidence indicating the currency of the idea of divine role-models in the ancient Near East, this potentially seductive hypothesis has been much criticized as anachronistic (cf. Lipinski 1986; Van der Toorn 1986: 496).

4. The migration of one-piece open-mould technology to Syria

At sometime in the eighteen to seventeenth centuries BC the one-piece open mould technology for manufacturing clay images was adopted across Syria (cf. Badre 1980). As it was used there almost exclusively for nude female images, without any sign of the wide range of motifs produced with it in Babylonia, this would appear to have been no more than a technological transfer. It put in the hands of the local Syrian religious authorities—or whoever—the means to mass-produce easily the local nude female image, which had already reached a remarkable degree of standardization by routine handmodelling by the second quarter of the second millennium BC. These flat silhouettes, easily handheld, were particularly typical of the Orontes Valley Region in western Syria. The Euphrates corridor, as so often, would have provided the means of transmission from Babylonia for the new technology and any iconographical associations that might have travelled along with it.

Significantly, already the Syrian nude female was associated with the local cult of Ishtar (Inanna), as is best illustrated at Ebla (Tell Mardikh), near Aleppo, in rubbish pits (*favissae*) in the so-called 'Sacred Area of Ishtar.' There the distinctive local handmade nude female images are conspicuous in Middle Bronze IB-IIA just before the emergence of mould-made images (*c.* 1850–1600 BC) (cf. Marchetti and Nigro 1997; Marchetti 2000). These distinctive figurines have elaborate heads and jewellery on the upper body; prominent navel and genitals (Plate 9). The arms are either bent, with hands cupping the breasts, or rendered as projecting stubs that may simply be an extreme stylization of the same pose. At Ebla these figurines were already broken when thrown into rubbish pits. The fact that a number in museum collections are complete may be explained at least in part by the fact that they were recovered by illicit excavations in the tombs of the region early in the last century during the construction of the Berlin to Baghdad railway.

These female images are associated with zoomorphic handmade figurines (equids and rams), perhaps token sacrificial victims, and two male types: equid and bull riders and seated figures holding axes or 'sceptres'. None of these anthropomorphic forms appear to be other than human suppliants or acolytes of Ishtar. There is a close correspondence in the males with the iconography of kings and royal officers depicted in the monumental art of this time in Syrian temples indicating that this is an aspect of *élite* cultic activity. The particular popularity of male imagery at a key stage of city-state formation in Syria, as during pristine state formation a millennium earlier in Sumer, may arise from the same social factors as were identified in the previous lecture. Whether they represented ancestors or living human beings is an open question.

5. Terracotta imagery in Canaan and the Egyptian connection

By the middle of the second millennium BC handmade stylized Syrian female figurines are evident at Taanach in northern Canaan (cf. Lapp 1964: 39–40; 1967: 35–7; 1969: 45). At much the same time, and again from the north, the use of the one-piece open mould technology was introduced for the manufacture of nude females in low relief on clay plaques in Canaan. These are the first anthropomorphic terracottas evident there for over half a millennium. This was the time when Egypt, from about 1650 BC, slowly established full imperial authority over Canaan (cf. Bunomovitz 1995). The terracottas of Canaan in the Late Bronze Age (*c*. 1550–1150 BC), like so many aspects of her material culture, may only be understood in terms of fashions and traditions emanating both from Syria in the north and from Egypt in the south.

As the Syro-Mesopotamian tradition has been described, it is only necessary here to introduce briefly the terracotta female imagery of Egypt, where the relevant goddess was Hathor, as Ishtar-Inanna was in Mesopotamia; but that should not be taken to indicate more than a common appeal particularly to women and their primary concerns in life. In her fully documented study *Votive Offerings to Hathor*, Geraldine Pinch (1993) has assembled the remarkable variety of artefactual evidence from Egypt, where conditions of preservation and, in general, recovery are so much better than in the Near East. They serve as a timely reminder of how much is lost from the material culture of popular worship in Canaan when organic materials do not survive. If used with due caution this much richer Egyptian evidence, textual as well as artefactual, allows the Canaanite terracottas to be assessed in terms of meaning and function in ways that would otherwise not be possible.

In Egypt, from the late third millennium BC, women prayed to traditional household deities, notably Hathor, as well as to family ancestors for help, particularly with the conception and safe delivery of children, above all sons. Such pleas were sometimes written on small images of nude women holding a child to epitomize the desired outcome. Throughout the second millennium BC female figurines in a variety of materials and types, were to be found not only in public shrines dedicated to Hathor, but also in household shrines and in burials. These were conceived as fertility charms in the first instance, then as amuletic protection in the rearing of infants. Thus their purpose, broadly stated, was to ensure the regular conception of children, their safe delivery and their survival as healthy offspring (cf. Meskell 1998). When offered by individuals or couples in rituals relating to Hathor (cf. Pinch 1993: 223), they were designed to endorse the continuity of family life. The emphasis on sexual characteristics is stronger in the earlier figurines than in the later ones (cf. Pinch 1993: 225).

The handmade terracotta female figurines made in Egypt in the earlier second millennium BC, variously found in burials, domestic and votive contexts, are a local phenomenon drawing upon traditions extending back deep into prehistory. By the late XVIIth and through the XVIIIth Dynasty (*c*. 1750–1250 BC) a series of mouldmade female images were placed in graves, but are more commonly found in houses. Their appearance when Egypt was ruled by a dynasty of Western Asiatic origin ('The Hyksos') may be significant, indicating once again just a technological transfer, this time from Canaan or Syria. The iconography it served to disseminate so much more readily was local Egyptian. In Egypt the imagery was not substantially modified through time. Some females still have elongated arms hanging down their sides, as traditional; others have the left arm bent across the breast, often holding either a lotus flower or a necklace counterpoise (*menit*), typically Egyptian features. The lotus appears also in Canaan in this context, significantly signalling the Egyptian connection.

Votive offerings in Egypt were distinguished, as might be anticipated in view of their well-known beliefs, by the absence of any rigid distinctions between benefits relating to life and to those of the after-life. Consequently the desired benefits were relevant not only to the cycle of life and death, but also to rebirth. This may not, of course, be assumed for the indigenous peoples of Canaan. The female terracotta images are not goddesses and their functions were predominantly associated with procreation. Children are occasionally shown in their arms. In Egyptian theology it was their intimate association with Hathor that was believed to charge them with *heka* ('magic'), one of the forces used by the creator god in making the world, and thus to empower them as talismans to ensure fertility (Pinch 1993: 126). In the absence of local evidence for the theology underlying Canaanite practice in the use of terracotta images this parallel is a useful indicator, providing a working hypothesis, rather than anything more definite in seeking to understand their Canaanite cousins.

6. Terracotta Plaques in Canaan during the Late Bronze Age *c.* 1650–1150 BC

The published archaeological evidence for the contexts and associations of nude female plaques in Canaan is, at present, seriously deficient by comparison with what is known of later assemblages. It is not clear, for instance, to what extent they were or were not regularly associated with the many contemporary handmade zoomorphic terracottas. In Egypt Hathor's familiar animal was the cow. Pioneer excavators in Palestine rarely recorded details of context; more recent excavators who did so in the field have often failed to publish the facts. Consequently, any general statements about Bronze Age terracottas in context are more provisional than is usually the case for the Iron Age, as will be clear in the third lecture.

In general, anthropomorphic terracottas would appear to be absent from the major sanctuaries and shrines of Late Bronze Age Canaan (cf. Ottoson 1980). Eighty-per-cent of graves are also without them (Keel and Uehlinger 1998: 100) and even when they appear in family graves there are only one or two of them. They are most often found in urban debris, at times battered and broken, recovered within areas of housing, storage and craft activities, from streets, pools and cisterns, in a pattern of distribution matched in Syro-Mesopotamia and later in Israel and Judah. All the terracotta humanoid imagery is female. The contemporary miniature male statuary is in metal and, compared with its virtual absence in the Iron Age, is relatively common and most evident in places of cultic activity (cf. Moorey and Fleming 1984; Keel and Uehlinger 1998: 97). This has been taken to strengthen the view that in Canaan female terracottas illustrate 'private piety' within the home, predominantly associated with women. There is some evidence that moulds for figurines were held by potters, who presumably manufactured and distributed positives from them together with household pottery (cf. Tufnell 1958: 90–1, 291–3, pl.49; Magrill and Middleton 2001).

The standard repertory was restricted to nude female relief plaques of two basic types which are widely evident in Canaan, whereas the relatively rare variants, often much cruder in appearance, are not. The state of current scholarship does not make it easy to discuss these two primary images with clarity and simplicity. Traditionally they have wholly conventional labels attached to them, based on the names of known goddesses. This prejudices from the outset attempts to identify the images and their possible functions, consequently it needs to be made immediately clear that no such clay plaque with an inscription on it from the area of Canaan has yet been published. Thus no objective evidence exists for confidently identifying the nude female(s) depicted on them.

Both types are shown full-frontal (*en face*). Two particular features distinguish them: the presence or absence of handheld or marginal floral attributes and their different feet positions. Those with floral attributes and the more distinctive Egyptianizing traits have their feet set to the side (Plate 10); those without floral attributes and more in the Syro-Mesopotamian mode have their feet together facing forward, sometimes clearly set on a podium (cf. Keel and Uehlinger 1998: 67; 203). Traditionally the lady with Egyptianizing floral attributes is termed *Qudshu* and the one without is termed *Astarte*. These two youthful goddesses, who appear labelled on Egyptian *stelae*, were of Asiatic origin. In the Egyptian pantheon only one or two specialized local adult deities were shown naked (cf. Goelet 1993). The primary examples are the sky-goddess Nut and her male counterpart, the earth god Neb. *Qudshu*, which as an epithet simply means 'holiness', is further exceptional in the Egyptian pantheon in being shown frontally rather than in profile on *stelae*, where her association with the ithyphallic Egyptian God Min endorses a particular connection with fertility (on *Qudshu* cf. Hadley 2000, passim).

The posture of these two females as shown is ambiguous, remembering that these plaques are not self-supporting, so she might be set up or held vertically, as if standing, or lain down flat or held horizontally, as if reclining. Miriam Tadmor (1982) sought to resolve the matter through their contrasting feet positions. When set together, she argued, the figure is recumbent on a bed or couch; when set to the side, she is standing as indeed she is sometimes shown on the back of her familiar animal on other objects (cf. Keel and Uehlinger 1998: 67). As the type, that with feet together, reclining, is without attributes (the *Astarte* type) it is commonly assumed that she is human. Miriam Tadmor, in fact identified this group as analogous to a type of Egyptian New Kingdom tomb figure commonly described as substitute concubines. Amongst Egyptologists, however, it is now accepted that this term is in need of reappraisal, not least since the objects in question are not confined to male burials (cf. Pinch 1983). Moreover, as has already been seen, the Old Babylonian nude female *stands* with her feet together facing forwards, at times on a podium, whilst contemporary depictions show *reclining* couples together on a bed with their feet in walking positions. Few, if any, of the Canaanite clay plaques of this general type, moreover, show any structural features, or vestiges of them, to indicate definitely a bed or couch in the way the Egyptian ones commonly do.

As the nude female *en face* with attributes (*Qudshu*) did not survive the fall of the Egyptian Empire in Canaan to confront image makers in Israel and Judah, as did the *Astarte* type without them, extended comment here is not required. That she passed with the Egyptian supremacy may be indicative of a special relationship to them and their cults. However, if she does represent a goddess, then she is an Asiatic one, not an Egyptian one in her nudity. It is difficult to see how progress will be made in further elucidating her status, divine, semi-divine or human and particular functions without some indication as to whether women of different cultural, racial, religious or social backgrounds had preferred this type to the other or whether the two types were each used in distinct and particular circumstances.

The *Astarte* type, a no less conventional academic label, represents much more closely the traditional Syro-Mesopotamian nude female who, it has been argued here was not a major deity. In Canaan hairstyles vary and some may indeed wear a headdress rather than just elaborately stacked hair; but then this had been a distinctive trait of nude females in the Mesopotamian tradition. The arm positions, in the absence of hand-held attributes, served other purposes. They are variously placed down her sides with hands touching the hips; bent at the elbows with the hands cupping or displaying the breasts; extended downwards with both hands placed on the abdomen, which is sometimes, if not invariably, swollen as if to indicate pregnancy; and with one hand placed down near the genitals, the other held over a breast. The feet are usually set together facing forward. As if to make the point more explicitly, it is this type that is, from time to time, shown suckling a child or children, occasionally depicted in uncanonical ways (cf. Keel and Uehlinger 1998: fig. 82).

It is such localized variants that serve to show how the presumed powers of these plaques when magically or ritually used, embraced all aspects of procreation, not serving merely as protection during or immediately after childbirth. As with their nearest Egyptian equivalents, any tendency to polarize their functions as primarily concerned with conception and birth on the one hand, sexual pleasure (whether male or female) on the other, is to misconceive their meanings. Such images were intended to reinforce or to endorse prayers by individuals, who considered themselves capable of establishing a personal relationship with a deity who was regarded as sufficiently interested in their daily lives to be approachable.

There are no compelling reasons to believe that they represent a goddess *per se* or a major cult image of one. It is more probable that they represent the messenger not the intended audience, either a human suppliant, perhaps ritually nude as appropriate in the circumstances, or propitious beings of a kind to be described later. As with the crucifix in Christianity, it may have been possible for cultic objects like these terracottas to have had efficacy and potency derived from a divine source without being a divine symbol. Indeed, that such objects had apotropaic or prophylactic roles in the lives of ordinary people, is suggested by the fact that the nude female in part, or as a complete figure, was depicted on pendants to be hung on necklaces or earrings made of precious materials for the *élite*. A whole series of small female plaques, pierced for suspension, were also made in dark blue glass in imitation of lapis lazuli (cf. Barag 1970, 188–91) to the *Astarte* pattern (Plate 11). The more Egyptianizing *Qudshu* type appears complete or in part on metal pendants (cf. McGovern 1985).

7. The Canaanite terracotta legacy in the first millennium BC (Iron Age)

The nude female in her Syro-Mesopotamian guise without Egyptianizing attributes was to epitomize a Canaanite legacy in the popular terracotta imagery in the Levant through to the collapse of the Achaemenid Persian

Empire after which the motif was Hellenized. Two particular aspects of the use of this motif at this time are instructive in any attempt to elucidate her role and to define the reasons why in the evolutionary stages of Israelite religion she was rejected in Judah, although evident to varying degrees elsewhere throughout the Levant. These aspects will be discussed in turn here, *first* her appearance on artefacts other than the handheld moulded plaques mass-produced in single open moulds; *second*, the variations in her appearance as she continued to be depicted on such plaques.

Clay models of free-standing structures or temple fittings in architectural shapes appear, though very rarely, already in the prehistoric villages of the Near East; but their continuous history does not, at present, appear to begin before the mature Bronze Age in the second millennium BC and, even then, they are far from common (cf. Bretschneider 1991a). An early appearance in the sixteenth century BC at Tell Muhammad Diyab in northeast Syria is in the Babylonian tradition (cf. Bachelot 1990). Here she was represented in pairs, alternating with countersunk panels, on the sides of a clay basin that appears to be a model of the large stone basins placed in Mesopotamian temples to represent the freshwater ocean believed to lie below the earth (cf. Black and Green 1992, figs. 18, 114). Their sides were carved in low relief with deities and other propitious supernatural beings. The use of identical pairs (and even more replications later) is not documented when the subjects are indisputably ranking goddesses.

Later in the second millennium BC in Syria terracotta models of various types of buildings are found in the residential quarters of towns, where they have usually been identified as models of the shrines of a family's ancestral deities used in household cults. They may most generally have served as offering stands in household shrines.

They are first evident in Canaan towards the end of the second millennium BC as the Egyptian imperial administration there passed into eclipse. Until then official cultic activity was characterized by large monumental temples on long established sites, as at places like Beth Shean, Hazor and Megiddo, and in lesser sanctuaries away from the major centres of the Egyptian administration. As this collapsed *c.* 1250–1050 BC, much more regional diversity is evident both in public shrines and in small scale cult activity, not so evident before, in domestic, industrial and extra-mural shrines. A distinctive feature of this phenomenon is the proliferation of terracotta stands in architectural shapes, serving not as incense stands so much as supports for bowls containing gifts or libations.

Keel and Uehlinger (1998: 154) have pointed out that their conservative shapes and decoration made 'sense sociologically, since most of these terracottas are associated with private or family piety.'

Amongst the more interesting appearances of nude females on such stands, where they are recurrent, is their direct association there with animals, most famously on one from Taanach, where she appears with lions (cf. Beck 1990). On an example from Pella in Jordan she is duplicated standing on a lion's head on either side of a doorway or aperture in a tower wall (cf. Potts *et al.* 1985). Her status here again is not self-evident. It may be doubted whether a major goddess, such as Astarte or Asherah, would be duplicated in such a subordinate role. They are more likely to represent her attendants or acolytes, or propitious supernatural beings in her service, with their mistress identified by the heads of her familiar animal.

This practice becomes more evident in the earlier Iron Age in regions peripheral to Israel and Judah. On model terracotta shrines, either represented in simplified three-dimensional forms or by plaque-like facades, mouldmade nude females are applied to the surface as if flanking the doorway to the cult room. This is now almost invariably without the image of deity within it. These have Babylonian precursors a millennium or so earlier; but, at this time, their currency has been explained particularly by their association with the Phoenicians, the cultural heirs of the Canaanites. Phoenician commercial activity by sea may explain their appearance in Cyprus, whilst the increasing use of camel caravans at this time carried Phoenician managed overland trade southwards to the Gulf of Aqaba and the Red Sea by routes east of the Jordan. There such model shrines are a distinctive feature of terracotta imagery in Ammon, Moab and Edom at a time of early state formation (cf. Culican 1976).

In an Edomite shrine, of the seventh century B.C. at Horvat Qitmit, near Beersheva, to which reference will be made in the next lecture, fragments of such models, including moulded nude female guardian images were found. Pirhiya Beck (1995, 123) characterized them as 'propitious beings' protecting the shrine and stressed their 'fertility aspect'. The common description of these models as house-shrines is evocative of the fact that even when they appear in isolated shrines remote from settlements they recall the major goddesses of hearth and home and the human concerns most relevant to them, not least in women's lives.

One of the distinctive features of the terracotta imagery of Israel and Judah, as will be examined in detail in the next lecture, is the rare appearance of male terracottas, in this case as horse-riders. In the Canaanite Late Bronze Age, as in contemporary Egypt, when the horse first appears in military contexts, the associated goddess is represented on the animal's back, nude and full-frontal (*en face*) with divine headdress and attributes (cf. Keel and Uehlinger 1998: 65-6, figs. 71-2). In the Iron Age, significantly, nude females, without divine headdresses, had a conspicuous role in the decoration of *élite* harness trappings in sheet metal and carved ivory. The two primary types are those already distinguished on the clay plaques of Canaan in the Late Bronze Age.

The nude female without floral attributes, the so-called *Astarte* type, is particularly associated with the *repoussé* decoration of metal harness-trappings attributed to Syrian production centres (cf. Kantor 1962). In this context she is represented in high relief. She again not only stands on lion's heads, but is also represented in a multiplicity of appearances on a single object in some cases (cf. Wicke 1999; Kyrieleis and Röllig 1988).

On the comparable fittings made of ivory in a distinctively Egypto-Phoenician style the nude females are carved in relief holding floral and animal attributes, whilst standing on lions (cf. Orchard 1967). Although the location of the workshops where these objects were made remains unknown, they were somewhere in modern Lebanon, Syria or south-east Turkey. These images, reminiscent of the Egyptianizing baked clay *Qudshu* plaques of Late Bronze Age Canaan, are combined on these equestrian ivory ornaments with such standard Egyptian good luck motifs as Eyes-of-Horus and Sphinxes. This is very reminiscent of the placing of nude females a millennium earlier alongside standard apotropaic symbols on Babylonian cylinder seals bearing inscriptions both for men and women. Here she protects equipment used by that most *élite* of male social groups, the chariot-warriors and cavalry.

It was, however, a continuing production of moulded terracotta plaques of females that carried this Canaanite female image deep into the Iron Age; but not without significant modifications in their iconography and their geographical distribution. In the Bronze Age the figure on the plaques had been set against so broad and flat a background that at times, as was noted earlier, it has been contentiously identified as a bed. From the twelfth century BC onwards, this background narrows, thus throwing into greater prominence first the head and then the whole body of the female until the background is virtually dispensed with. Although such plaques become less common in the southern Levant, they were not wholly eclipsed, except in Judah. Now, intermittently the women hold suckling infants (cf. Kletter 1996, fig.11). Their primary distribution was in Philistia and adjacent areas, as well as northwards up the coast to the plain of Esdraelon and beyond (cf. Kletter 1996: 268-80).

The most conspicuous novelty in this continuing tradition is the appearance of females, now dressed and veiled with varying details of costume, hairstyles and jewellery, united only in holding a disc-shaped object. Kletter's (1996: 34–5) census of them has located most in Transjordan. Their contexts are generally domestic. Three-dimensional standing females in terracotta from shrines in Cyprus and Phoenicia, also dressed, indicate that the disk is most often, if not invariably, a tambourine rather than such suggested alternatives as flat bread-loaves or cakes, or even solar disks. Dancing and music had been intimately associated with cult activities since prehistory. One anomalous image appears to show a hermaphrodite (cf. Beck 1999). If these individuals are musicians, they are an indicator of corporate worship in this range of terracottas, again perhaps indicative of the natural rather than the supernatural identities of the figures depicted.

From the outset of the Iron Age, notably amongst the intrusive Philistine communities with their Aegean background (cf. Schmitt 1999), handmade terracottas had represented individual human beings coming together to celebrate, to mourn and to worship in the company of musicians. This is in marked contrast to the self-referential individualized world of the moulded plaques, with their single female images. They most probably served as *talismans*, magical figurines conceived as benefiting their owners, rather than as *icons* depicting sacred images. Primarily, they epitomized female piety, individual rather than communal, focused on a deity in the official state pantheon, whose identity is not explicit in their imagery as it represents an intermediary between suppliant and deity, rather than the deity herself.

It was in Cyprus, in particular, that in the second quarter of the first millennium B.C. free-standing, three-dimensional anthropomorphic terracottas were deposited in sanctuaries, often in considerable numbers. Mythological terracotta figurines are rare (cf. Reyes 1994: 34–5; nn.60–70). Their costume, postures and offerings indicate human suppliants. Associated votive scenes of daily life, as in Phoenicia, modelled in terracotta, evoke the realities of the world in which the suppliants lived. As will be explored in the final lecture, the terracottas of Israel and Judah, both in their technology and imagery, share more with this world of Cypriot and Phoenician terracottas than with those of the Canaanite tradition.

The final phase of that tradition as exemplified by the moulded plaques was contemporary with the Achaemenid Persian Empire in Syro-Mesopotamia (*c.* 550–350 BC). They are particularly well represented in

PLATE 5

Two handmade terracotta suppliants or worshippers; excavated at Kish in Iraq; *c.* 2100 BC; 7.6 cm, 8.6 cm (1927.3282; 1931.163).

Babylonian terracotta mouldmade plaque of the upper part of a deity or her cult image; source unknown; c. 1900–1750 BC; 10 cm high. (1949.920).

PLATE 7

Babylonian terracotta mouldmade plaque of a nude female standing on a podium; source unknown; *c.* 1900–1750 BC; 12 cm high (1924.499).

PLATE 8

Mouldmade terracotta model bed with reclining nude female; perhaps from southwest Iran; c. 1500–1200 BC; 13 cm long (1965.757).

PLATE 9

Handmade Syrian Nude Female terracotta figurine with gold earrings and navel plug; source unknown; late third to early second millennium BC; 15.3 cm long (1933.1182).

PLATE 10

Mouldmade terracotta 'Qudshu' plaque; from Gezer in Israel; *c.* 1300 BC; 12 cm long (1912.621).

PLATE 11

Mouldmade blue glass pendant in the shape of an 'Astarte' plaque; excavated at Tell ed-Duweir (Lachish in Israel; 5.5 cm long (1955.501). (Print from original excavation negative).

PLATE 12

Handmade terracotta female 'pillar-figurines'; from various sites in Syria; seventh century BC; 13.5 cm; 10.3 cm; 13.9 cm; 12.5 cm high (1913.447; 1913.634; 1914.795; 1914.796).

Japanese excavations of a simple settlement at Tell Mastuma, near Aleppo, in Syria (cf. Nishiyama and Yoshizawa 1997). They revealed many such plaques in a broken state. Two types were directly associated in both ash-pits and in general domestic rubbish. Some are the traditional nude females without attributes, but others wear the distinctive 'Persian Robe' with its long sleeves, previously unknown in Near Eastern costume, and its characteristic multiple vertical folds. These draped females hold a lotus (?) flower between their breasts, which were sometimes, if not invariably, exposed. Their embroidered robes and jewellery have links with the older iconography of Inanna-Ishtar in Syro-Mesopotamia (cf. Opificius 1998).

These plaques are variously marked with red paint; a colour popularly signifying fertility in some parts of the Arab World to this day. A pattern of breakage has the appearance of being deliberate: the draped females are generally broken at the neck; the nude females at neck, waist and legs in relatively even numbers. Handmodelled miniature male riders in the distinctive Median costume, its trousers ideal for the purpose, were found together with these female plaques (cf. Moorey 2000).

The nude females, though reported in slightly larger numbers than the draped ones, were not dominant. What the difference indicates here is not clear. Is this a case of dress as a declaration of ethnic identity or of the adoption by local Syrian women of 'Persian' costume in a quest for the status conferred by it? Certainly, neither clay plaques nor terracotta images are features of popular religion amongst the Iranian-speaking peoples in their homelands. On typical Achaemenid Persian seals and embroidered textiles dressed women are shown in acts of worship in domestic settings, placed on either side of an incense burner symbolic of the deity (cf. Moorey 2002). Some, as on these clay plaques, may expose their breasts. Perhaps more than with any of the other plaques considered in this lecture, the carefully reported disposal practices at Tell Mastuma may be taken to indicate vehicles of magic that were manipulated and then disposed of in rituals intended to produce, prevent or reverse specific situations with the aid of a major local goddess. There is nothing to indicate that these are representations of goddesses or their cult statues. Some may be ritually nude in the local Syrian tradition, others dressed according to the fashions of the Iranian-speaking peoples; but both represent either human suppliants themselves or beneficent spirits acting as intermediaries between deity and woman in the tradition established in Babylonia and Syria in the earlier second millennium BC.

The free-standing, handmade Iron Age Judean terracottas anthropomorphic, zoomorphic and inanimate in form, are in striking contrast to the tradition of mouldmade, hand-held plaques, whose history has been traced here through to their eclipse by the last quarter of the first millennium BC. The plaques appear to have been rejected in Judah, though to some extent evident in Israel, as elsewhere in the Levant and Cyprus. Whether they were directly replaced in Judah by the free-standing female pillar figurines or not will be a primary question in the final lecture.

III

Terracotta Imagery in Israel and Judah under the Divided Monarchy (*c.* 925–586 BC)

1. Israelite goddesses: terracotta figurines

In 1998 the British Museum published a book of essays, by various authors, under the title *Ancient Goddesses: the Myths and the Evidence* (Goodison and Morris (eds.)). It was designed as a wide-ranging critical examination of the 'Universal Mother Goddess Hypothesis', described in the first lecture. It is likely that some at least amongst its readers would have been surprised to find there, set alongside essays on the goddesses of ancient Egypt, Babylonia and Assyria, Greece, Rome and prehistoric Europe, one on 'Goddesses in Early Israelite Religion' by Karel van der Toorn, who pointed out that

> few scholars would be ready to accept the notion of one Hebrew Goddess, but the importance of various goddesses amongst the Israelites is widely recognized ... In the day-to-day devotion of ordinary people, goddesses seem to have played a role inversely proportional to their official importance.

That such a chapter is now taken for granted in such a book, as it would not have been less than a generation ago, maybe accounted for largely by the vigorous and ongoing academic debate generated over the last thirty years by the eighth century BC inscriptions found in modern Israel at Khirbet el-Qom and Kuntillet 'Ajrud, mentioned early in the first lecture, that include the phrase 'Yahweh (and) his asherah' (cf. Hadley 2000).

These inscriptions not only dramatically opened up the whole question of the role of the worship of goddesses of Canaanite origin in the states of Israel and Judah; but also of the place of women in that worship. Both are subjects notoriously marginalized in the Old Testament and potentially visible primarily in the archaeological record in numerous free-standing, largely handmodelled, pillar-shaped female terracotta figurines with pendulous breasts (Plate 14). These have become known amongst archaeologists from their form and distribution as 'Judean Pillar Figurines' (cf. Kletter 1996) and increasingly amongst Old Testament scholars as 'Asherahs', images of the Canaanite Goddess of that name (cf. van der Toorn 1998: 91–95), whose symbol was wooden, perhaps closely resembling a tree or tree-trunk, referred to by the same word. In the Canaanite pantheon, best known from texts found at Ugarit (modern Ras Shamra) in Syria, she was the wife of El, the head of the local pantheon, and mother of the gods. The evident popularity of such miniature clay images in Judah, particularly, in the eighth and seventh centuries BC has been increasingly taken to indicate the popularity of her cult at this time (cf. Dever 1996: 46 for endorsement; Kletter 1996, *passim*; Hadley 2000: 204, for more sceptical assessments). No figurine of this, or any other anthropomorphic form, has yet been published with an inscription referring to a deity on its painted surface. Any attribution is then necessarily provisional, whether sacred or profane. Three aspects, in particular, of current approaches to these clay female statuettes, are open to question:

First, there is the marked tendency to isolate them from the other types of terracottas within the repertory to which they belonged, most notably the male horse-riders. Their appearance is the more remarkable both on account of the novelty of the subject at the time and the relative rarity of male terracottas in the ancient Near East at all times. In Late Bronze Age Canaan miniature male votive statuary was made of metal and, so far as the archaeological record goes, was a relatively rare phenomenon associated with shrines and temples in marked contrast to the numerous nude female terracotta plaques, described in the previous lecture, recovered from various urban contexts and from graves. If the Iron Age females are to be associated with a goddess, what then of the males? What also of the numerous zoomorphic terracottas and much rarer models of inanimate objects sometimes found together with the humanoid forms?

Second, there is a recurrent absence of attention to parallel combinations of pillar-shaped female and equestrian male terracottas in contemporary contexts in Transjordan, Syria and Cyprus (Plates 12–13). This is particularly striking in respect of Cyprus, where the evidence is well published and already plentiful (cf. Young and Young 1955). The range and quantity of painted terracotta imagery in Iron Age Cypriot sanctuaries and shrines is remarkable. As Reyes (1994: 34) recently commented 'recognizably mythological figures appear infrequently' amongst them; but what are generally regarded as male or female human suppliants or worshippers are innumerable. Votive figurines, in themselves, do not by their sex necessarily provide clues to the deity in whose honour they were deposited at those shrines in Cyprus where inscriptions reveal the identity of the deity in question. Where both males and females appear, it might be to honour either a god or a goddess.

Third, here the discussion moves on to more contentious ground, broached in my opening lecture. Ethnographic analogies recurrently reveal that terracotta figurines do not have to conform to a common expectation for them to be representations of supernatural beings or forces rather than living human beings acting as votaries or dead human beings as ancestors or ghosts. Moreover, when placed in graves, as from time to time the 'Judean Pillar Figurines' were, ethnographic parallels indicate that they have a number of possible roles, but that they are rarely, if ever, divine images in such contexts. They more often relate to ancestor worship (cf. Ucko 1962: 45–48; 1968: 420–43). Grave-goods, however, need not be special cases, they may simply be assemblages of things used by the deceased in life provided for use in the hereafter (cf. Kletter 1996: 58, n.3).

There are no *explicit* references to these miniature images in the Old Testament. They used to be popularly associated with the biblical *teraphim* (cf. *Genesis* 31: 19; I *Samuel* 19: 13–17); but these images would appear to have been made of materials other than clay and, to judge from I *Samuel* (19: 13–17), when Michal uses them to conceal the escape of David from Saul's wrath, were life-size or nearly so at least in some cases. The same disparity of medium and scale would also appear to rule out identity with the *asherim*, particularly mentioned in *Chronicles* (cf. Hadley 2000: 201). *Jeremiah* 44: 19 is rather less easily disposed of, particularly in such free translations as that given by *The Jerusalem Bible*. Here Jeremiah refers to the Jewish community in Egypt after the destruction of Jerusalem:

> the women added, when we offer incense to the Queen of Heaven and pour libations in her honour, do you think we make cakes for her with her features on them, and pour libations to her, without our husband's knowledge?

This short passage is instructive in various ways:

First, it calls to our attention how much is lost to archaeology through the use of organic materials in the practice of family religious rituals by ordinary people. In climates like that of Egypt, where they more readily endure, this is very evident amongst the surviving range of offerings to Hathor, the goddess of women (cf. Pinch 1993).

Second, it reminds us of the involvement of men, albeit indirectly, in domestic worship. This may be made explicit by the male terracottas of Israel and Judah, if they represented natural not supernatural beings.

Third, it demonstrates how, even when a Biblical reference is available, it may all too often raise as many questions as it answers. The goddess here is cited by a title not a name, leaving unclear whether the Babylonian goddess Ishtar (familiar from the last lecture) might be implied, as some scholars have suggested (cf. Lipinski 1986: 94), rather than a local goddess (Keel and Uehlinger 1998: 338–41). Then, to complicate the matter further, the phrase rendered 'to fashion her' or 'to make an image of her', has been identified as a possible later explanatory addition. Even so, it is not possible to say with any certainty from the Hebrew precisely what is meant, as the verb only occurs once elsewhere, and then not in the same theme. It thus remains open to question whether the cake itself was a mouldmade female image or whether her image or symbol was incised or stamped onto it (Professor Hugh Williamson: personal communication). In a parallel passage in *Jeremiah* 7: 18 there is no reference to features (Cf. Keel and Uehlinger 1998, 340, fig.32 for a questionable parallel to a clay bread stamp).

In any study of terracottas it is important to remember that Israel had a much more heterogeneous population than Judah, with 'Israelites' in the highlands, 'Canaanites' in the lowlands. As geography dictated Israel was affected first by the imperial aspirations of Assyria, but her impact on Judah, when it came, was more sudden and radical, opening her up in an unprecedented way in the later eighth century BC to external contacts. Marked cultural contrasts between the two should not be underestimated. Nor should the fact that official religion was focused on Yahweh in both states be taken to indicate a necessary identity of cult objects and religious practices in homes and workplaces in both kingdoms.

2. The Emergence of Free-standing Terracottas in Israel and Judah

Archaeological evidence for terracottas in Israel and Judah in the first quarter of the first millennium BC remains elusive. As the intensity of research through controlled excavations proceeds, this contrast with other parts of the Levant tends to suggest that this is an indicator of real absence. At the outset of the Iron Age (*c*. 1200–1000 BC) research designed to explain the emergence of the 'People of Israel' in the highlands of Canaan has stimulated a rare concentration in Near Eastern archaeology on rural surface surveys and non-urban settlements. Terracotta images, significantly, have not yet been reported from them (cf. Finkelstein 1995). Nor are they any more evident yet at the time of the United Monarchy.

In the immediately subsequent stages of state development in Israel and Judah from the ninth century onwards they emerge rarely, if at all, in the few official shrines or sanctuaries so far excavated. In the north at Tel Dan, a set of massive stone foundations has been identified as the high-place founded by Jeroboam I, the former Solomonic official, who revolted against Solomon's successor Rehoboam and then promoted official sanctuaries at Bethel and Dan to deflect religious loyalties in the northern state of Israel away from Jerusalem in Judah (cf. Biran 1994: 159–233). Very few terracottas have been reported from it. In the south the shrine located in the citadel at Tel Arad did not yield any terracottas, but the fort of which it was a part did (cf. Holladay 1987). This rarity of terracottas in state-sponsored shrines is comparable in general to the situation earlier in Late Bronze Age Canaan (cf. Ottoson 1980).

Terracottas were primarily domestic objects in Israel and Judah, as they had been in Canaan. Once they were no longer needed, they were disposed of exactly like pottery vessels. Archaeologists recover terracottas, often battered and broken, from houses, cisterns and pools, streets and gateways, and from workplaces, usually in ordinary rubbish deposits. Only those placed in graves are most often recovered in good condition. In houses at this time the ground floor area was used to accommodate animals and stores, whilst the family accommodation, when not in the courtyard or on the flat roof, would have been on the first floor. This is almost invariably found collapsed, together with its contents, randomly into the lower spaces, thus destroying all evidence for the original association of groups of household equipment. This explains why finds of terracottas in concentrations, which might be indicative of the original uses and associations of diverse types, are so rare in the archaeological record. When they occur, they acquire a possibly disproportionate significance in attempts to elucidate the meanings and functions of individual types.

3. Two key contexts: Cave I (Ophel), Jerusalem (Judah) and area E-257, Samaria (Israel)

This lecture will be no exception. It is divided into two sections treating contexts first and then types of figurines. It will deal initially with associations of diverse terracottas in two major contexts, one in Judah, the other in Israel. Cave I on the slopes of Ophel in East Jerusalem was excavated in the final season of the Kenyon excavations there in 1967. The far less well-known area E-207 at Samaria in ancient Israel, was excavated by Sukenik as a member of the Crowfoot expedition in the early 1930s, when Kathleen Kenyon served her apprenticeship in Palestinian archaeology on the same expedition. She was subsequently to be responsible for much of the ceramic study on which the internal site chronology was based.

Cave I on the south-east hill (Ophel) in Jerusalem was man-made, measuring originally about 8.12 metres deep and 4.2 metres wide. It was cut for use as a tomb. It was divided by a wall extending from a central pillar of rock. It had been carved into a rock scarp on the lower slopes of Ophel, some way north of the Gihon Spring, where it was on the lower of two rock terraces. The upper one had supported city walls in the Bronze and Iron Ages; the lower accommodated extra-mural domestic structures, a paved road and water-gullies (cf. Franken and Steiner 1990; Eshel and Prag 1995).

The life-history of the original Iron Age tomb had been obscured by later features. It may originally have been the standard type of tomb, with a front hall off which led two chambers, one of which may have had benches on which the dead were laid. Some Iron Age tombs have amongst their burial offerings baked clay female and animal or bird figurines, as well as miniature model seats (cf. Eshel and Prag 1995: 209); but, as this one was judged to have been cleared out at some time before being put to secondary use, none of the surviving figurines would appear to have been mortuary equipment.

Indeed, as Kay Prag (Eshel and Prag 1995: 215) has pointed out in her summary of the contents as recorded during excavation, 'there is nothing in the materials found ... which cannot be interpreted as deriving from domestic contexts, and most of the objects suggest very standard processes. It is the quantities found in one deposit that are remarkable.' Whereas all the figurines were broken, a large number of complete pots as well as innumerable sherds were recovered. At least 2400 pottery vessels were listed, some of which bore incised marks, perhaps made at the time of manufacture. Others bore personal names incised after firing. They are either property marks or names of those making offerings in them (cf. Prigneaud 1978). Some of the other bowls and cooking pots contained animal bones. Sixty-one anthropomorphic and zoomorphic terracotta figurines were listed from within the Cave and nineteen from the entrance area ('porch'). Out of a group of twenty-six objects listed separately as 'cult-equipment', all but four were found in the body of the Cave. They included six rattles, seven fragmentary miniatures in baked clay of chairs or couches, and part of at least one building model (Plate 16). There was one complete and possibly three fragmentary ceramic incense stands and seven fragments of pedestal feet or bases for such objects.

Eshel (in Eshel and Prag 1995: 22), in his detailed comparative analysis by function and by type of the Cave I pottery, emphasized the absence of 'cultic pottery types' in any way similar to those recovered from area E-207 at Samaria in association with comparable domestic wares (to be considered below). His conclusion corresponds closely with Prag's appraisal when he notes that 'the functional character which emerges from this statistical analysis points to normal household and domestic use'. The figurines associated with this pottery are not an obstacle to this proposal. Diana Gilbert-Peretz (1996: 39) argued in her report on the terracottas found during Shiloh's 'City of David' excavations that their distribution within the site was uniform. 'Moreover', she points out, 'such a uniform distribution pattern has been found at other excavated sites in Judah. Thus attempts to relate them to specific ritual places were unfounded ... figurines have appeared in similar concentrations in both residential buildings and locations considered to be ritual sites, such as Kenyon's Cave I.'

However, the contents of this Cave, as found, may not be exceptional by comparison with these residential findspots, if its contents were simply a combination of material from the occupation of the Cave, after it had ceased to be a tomb, and of domestic debris from elsewhere dumped in it. Indeed, Franken (1995: 239) has proposed that 'when the new town was built, the whole site was dumped with debris to serve as foundations for a road'. Kletter (1996: 95), in his special study of the female Judean Pillar Figurines, has pointed out that they are very often associated with domestic pottery in excavations.

Kenyon also excavated two other so-called 'cave deposits' (II and III) in the vicinity of Cave I; but, by comparison with it, they are rather more accurately described as rock niches. Cave II yielded four figurines and fragments of cult apparatus with two hundred and eighty-eight pots.

Cave III contained only one figurine and seventy-nine pots (cf. Eshel and Prag 1995: 209–20). A further group, known simply as Deposit IV, included thirty-nine pots and a fragment of a cultic type of vessel ('chalice').

The best known explanation for the origins of the contents of Cave I, since it was Kenyon's own, argued both in her academic and her popular accounts, was that it had been a special repository for objects used in cultic activities so as to prevent their reuse for profane purposes (*favissa*). She based this interpretation on the fact that she thought she had found an altar-base on the upper terrace close to Cave I, associated with two stone 'sacred pillars' (*mazzeboth*) below it on the terrace. Subsequent research has, however, thrown serious doubts on these identifications. Exactly similar pillars were routine structural elements elsewhere on Ophel (as at other Iron Age sites) and are not independent evidence for identifying the enigmatic stone feature on the terrace above them as an altar-base. This does not, of course, invalidate the *favissa* hypothesis completely, as there may be an undiscovered shrine elsewhere in the vicinity from which these artefacts might have come. At present, however, arguments of probability indicate that these associated groups are not from places exclusively used for cultic purposes; but from residential areas where cult practices were integrated with the routines of daily life whether in individual households or communally.

In Cave I the anthropomorphic figurines were found only in the interior, while the animal figurines were in the entrance or on the floors of rooms outside the Cave as well as in it. All were broken. Holland (1977: 137) listed eighty-four examples, embracing female pillar figurines, all hand modelled but some with solid, others with hollow bodies, solid horses and male riders; solid birds and miscellaneous solid animals. There seems no good reason, as Holland and others have done, to separate the animate miniature forms from the inanimate (furniture and buildings), calling the latter 'cult apparatus' which, in a sense, all terracotta miniatures were. In any attempt to elucidate figurine functions the miniaturization of anthropomorphic forms, goods and chattels, animate and inanimate, is the unifying characteristic whether or not they were used together or separately for cult or ritual purposes.

As absolute chronologies for pottery in Judah during the eighth and seventh centuries BC (Iron Age IIC) remain fluid, precise dating of these deposits on Ophel is hardly possible. Franken and Steiner (1990) proposed that the pottery in Caves II and III was earlier than that in Cave I; the former they dated *c*. 800 BC, the latter 750–700 BC. Eshel, in the analysis already noted, lowered the dating of the pottery in Caves I and II to about 700–650 BC. Close dating is of most concern to those who would wish to interpret the contents of Cave I, particularly, as direct evidence for the destruction of unorthodox popular shrines during the religious reforms of King Josiah (c. 640–609 BC). Dever, particularly, has argued in this connection that 'it is entirely reasonable to see, reflected in the cache of figurines the *Sitz-im-Leben* of his reforms. According to II *Kings* 23 the shrines of Asherah (Ashtoreth) and other deities on the Temple Mount were dismantled, their paraphernalia smashed and the debris thrown into the Kidron Valley' (Dever 1991: 64–5).

These archaeological assemblages, however, do not offer much correspondence to the despoilment reported in *Kings*: '....from the Temple of Yahweh he (Josiah) removed the sacred pole right out of Jerusalem to the wadi Kidron, and in the Wadi Kidron he burnt it: to ashes and threw its ashes on the common burying-ground' (*II Kings*: 23: 4–7). Perhaps more relevant to any understanding of the battered terracottas and their associated household pottery is Tappy's (1998: 88) suggestion that this may have been a vindictive choice reflecting the special relationship of commoners with the cult of Asherah.

It is more plausible to interpret the various Ophel assemblages as the material remnants of rituals preformed by the common people in family groups or communally. Even if we accept that they were related to the cult of Asherah, they need not have had any close affinity to major images in state-sponsored cults. The distinctive combination of ordinary household ceramics, perhaps indicating feasts, with almost invariably broken terracottas of the primary types in varying proportions, appears to document patterns of worship rather different from those epitomized by the Canaanite handheld terracotta plaques. They would appear to focus an individual woman's piety upon the goddess of most concern to her in more private circumstances.

The only other archaeological assemblage in anyway truly comparable, at present, to that in Jerusalem Cave I was found seventy years ago in area E-207 at Samaria in ancient Israel (cf. Crowfoot *et al.* 1942: 23–4; 1957: 75–82; Holladay 1987). It was concisely published without detailed drawings or photographs of the site when under excavation. This is best described as a moated island of rock, located just outside the easternmost extension of the Israelite fortifications at Samaria and thus, like Cave I, in an extra-mural location. Here a trench, some 3.5 metres deep and some 6 metres wide at the top (4 metres at the bottom), had been cut into the bedrock to enclose an area 30 × 26 × 26 metres, with an entrance causeway 2.4 metres wide. Only a small part of the enclosed area was excavated. No traces of structures were revealed, as the top of the rock was close to the surface and many later disturbances were evident in it. At one point a pathway led up to a cave, found empty, but with its blocking extant.

The numerous small finds recovered by the excavators came from the ditch of which about three-quarters was cleared. They date to the seventh century BC (Samaria: Ceramic Period VI). This debris is assumed to have come from corporate rituals carried out within the enclosed area. Terracottas were recovered amongst this pottery:

> Twenty-three female, two male, thirty-four horses, about eighty-three bovines, one camel, one sheep, one donkey and the bodies of more than twenty animals too broken to identify, as well as baskets of smaller fragments ... a few plaque figures ... none ... of pillar base types are complete ... in general only the heads ... survive .. (with) eyes ... (which are) never the disk "buttons" seen on male heads and the "animals" (Crowfoot *et al.*, 1942: 76).

Amongst the pottery recovered here vessels for the preparation and eating of food and for drinking were conspicuous; whilst 'several baskets-full' of lamps were recorded. They were generally of the open shell-shaped types without multi-spouted or pedestal forms. Eshel has provided a functional and typological study of this ceramic assemblage comprising some eight hundred pots. A dominant pottery sub-group was 'mainly made up of cultic pottery types-chalices, cups and saucers, portable braziers, *kernoi*, rattles, etc. ... All these unusual varieties and quantities of cultic items, make up a dominant functional feature which is very different from the two Jerusalem groups' (i.e. from Caves I and II) (Eshel and Prag 1995: 23). He compared this group to finds from an Edomite shrine at Horvat Qitmit in southern Israel, not then fully published, to which I shall return. As in Cave I, the Samaria deposit contained pottery vessels with personal names incised on them after firing (Birnbaum in Crowfoot *et al.* 1957, 11–19, 21–25).

Cave I in Jerusalem and Samaria E-207 have certain shared features apart from their extra-mural location. Both are particularly characterized by numerous terracotta figurines. These are entirely lacking or absent in statistically significant numbers from the state-sponsored altars, cult-platforms, and shrines of Israel and Judah so far excavated (cf. Nakhai 1994; Stern 2001). Moreover, both had far larger numbers of vessels for serving food and drink than might be explained by token offerings of consumables, allowing that pottery was commoner in Cave I.

It is perhaps significant that neither had any of the contemporary tall limestone 'incense-altars' known elsewhere at this time, although each had at least one tall, fenestrated clay cult-stand (Holland 1977, fig. 9: 23). In view of the domestic origin argued here for the Cave I deposit, it is also interesting to note that it did contain two miniature stone cuboid altars or 'incense-burners' of the type usually found in houses (Holland 1977, fig. 9: 21–2). The lamps at Samaria are worth special attention, as they would appear to imply use at night or in a situation, like a cave, where artificial lighting would be called for.

Holladay (1987: 280) has argued that both deposits were 'independently witness to surprisingly short periods of intense active use.' At Samaria this might have been the case; but in Jerusalem, if the interpretation of Cave I offered here is viable, this is not self-evident. Keel and Uehlinger (1998: 348–9) described these two contexts as 'underworld types of milieu', focusing on the caves in both cases as functionally similar and used by men and women. They explain them thus: 'the massive use of cooking, eating and drinking utensils make it probable that these sites were used for the so-called *marzē^{a}h*, sacral meals related to the Canaanite El religion' (cf. *Amos* 6: 7; *Jeremiah* 16: 5). This hypothesis not only places special emphasis on the role of the cave in each case, and in neither is it explicitly the focus of the activities implied by the material remains; but it also has now to be confronted with Eshel's distinction between the Cave I and E-207 ceramic assemblages and by the general relevance of the figurines to such a setting.

Holladay (1987) also called attention to two other small 'cult-areas' associated with caves. At Tell en-Nasbeh two female pillar figurines, a horse-and-rider and a model chair were found with a pottery 'chalice' outside an extra-mural cave, whilst at Tell Beit Mirsim a cave opened into a courtyard, with two stone-lined basins or wine-presses, where two female pillar figurines and two clay animals were also found. It is not evident, certainly in Jerusalem, that the cave itself was a place of devotion, though Franken (1995: 239–40), highlighting potential magical roles for the figurines, has interpreted it thus, in the light of ethnographical parallels, as 'the scene of a sorcerer's activities.'

In assessing the role of Cave I, after its evident initial use as a tomb, and of the caves elsewhere, the routine use of caves in all ages in this region as dwellings, stores, stables, byres and workplaces needs always to be borne in mind. Kletter's conclusion, following his exhaustive assessment of Judean Pillar Figurines, that 'most of the JPFs are related to domestic (private) contexts', would accommodate the deposits of Cave I as interpreted here. It is E-207, significantly perhaps in Israel rather than in Judah, that is distinctive in being more suggestive of communal activities in a clearly non-domestic setting.

4. The repertory of Judean terracottas in the eighth and seventh Centuries BC

It is still difficult to date accurately, as it is to explain, the re-emergence in the mature Iron Age, during the eighth century BC, of handmade free-standing clay anthropomorphic figurines together with models of furniture and rare buildings. The latter had been unknown in the region since the third millennium BC. Many, if not all, had been whitewashed with details painted on this background in black and red, ochre and yellow paint. Animal figurines made by hand, however, had not suffered so long an eclipse, surviving through the Canaanite Late Bronze Age and then into the Iron Age. In Judah the moulded female clay plaques of the Canaanite tradition, discussed in the previous lecture, are not evident, suggesting a rejection of whatever they had represented. They do occur sporadically in Israel, as in E-207 at Samaria, and remain a primary type elsewhere in the Levant and Cyprus into the Achaemenid Persian Empire.

The first appearance of the new types may only be tentatively dated at present to sometime in the first half of the eighth century BC. Many of the settlements in Israel destroyed by Assyrian invaders in 732–30 and 720 BC have few solid, handmodelled clay figurines in the debris (cf. Kletter 1996: 40–42). But in those settlements which flourished in the seventh century BC, local types of female pillar figurines are common.

In their detailed studies of seal designs in the Divided Monarchy during the eighth century BC Keel and Uehlinger (1998: 249ff.) have shown how heavily they were influenced by those of Phoenicia and Syria. Moreover, some of the earliest known female pillar figurines occur at northern sites like Tell Farah (North) (cf. Holladay 1987: 280). This may reinforce the suggestion that the return of handmade, primarily solid, free-standing clay miniatures to the southern Levant had its source in the north. Syria had her own traditions of free-standing, handmodelled, solid pillar-shaped female figurines and horse-riders in the rather crude so-called 'snowman' technique at the time of the Assyrian invasions of Israel southwards through Syria in the second half of the eighth century BC (Cf. Tell Afis: D'Amore 1998) (Plates 12–13). The first appearance of mould-made heads on handmodelled bodies in Syria, as on one type of Judean female pillar figurines, has yet to be established; but a significant number of mouldmade heads were found at Tell Rifa'at in Syria in the seventh century BC (Cf. Novaka 1979: 149–53).

The wide influence of Phoenician terracottas has already been noted. The Phoenicians used the potter's wheel to create cone-shaped hollow lower bodies for free-standing female figurines. This feature is evident on some Judean types. They also employed two-piece moulding, which is not. However, the Phoenicians did manufacture clay tomb models portraying scenes from daily life, which illustrate the currency amongst them of the handmodelling of solid three-dimensional images (cf. Kletter 1996: 282, fig.9). The intimate relationship of the Phoenicians with Cyprus, reflected there in many crafts, makes attribution of distinctive shared traits difficult. The practice of covering the entire figure with white-wash, characteristic of many Judean female figurines, as a base for adding details in various colours of paint, is also familiar in the manufacture of terracottas in Cyprus between about 850 and 600 BC (Cf. Young and Young 1955; Franken 1995: 234). Methods of manufacture in Cyprus also to some degree parallel those in Judah, as do the combination of female standing and male riding images (cf. Young and Young, 1955).

These free-standing, three-dimensional anthropomorphic, zoomorphic and inanimate miniatures have a performative potential last seen in the prehistoric and early historic periods in marked contrast to the moulded plaques. It is then hardly surprising that they have been, and continue to be, categorized as children's playthings by many commentators, not least in popular surveys of daily life in Old Testament times. Huizinga's (1980: 14) classic study, referred to earlier, of *Homo Ludens* defined the basic problem explicitly: 'passing from children's games to the sacred performances in archaic culture, we find there is more of a mental effort "at play" in the latter, though it is excessively difficult to define.'

It is accepted here that some of these images may at times have served as children's playthings; but that this was the least significant aspect of their potential roles in daily life. As assemblages and contexts indicate, these miniature images were the instruments through which the people at large in their own communities approached supernatural powers for aid and comfort in ways that were, presumably, thought by them to be acceptable to the supernatural powers thus petitioned. Unfortunately, they have survived without the verbal complements that animated and conveyed their messages in ritual acts. Their absence is made particularly evident if they are compared with those contemporary Neo-Assyrian magical clay figurines which have survived not only inscribed with their identities and apotropaic functions, but sometimes still *in situ* in specially protected foundation deposits at appropriate points in buildings. Moreover, they are also documented by the survival of the relevant 'spells' recorded on clay tablets (cf. Wiggermann 1986).

The terracottas of Israel and Judah in the eighth and seventh centuries are varied. At the heart of this repertory, and by far the most discussed, are the standing female images with their exaggerated breasts and columnar lower bodies, sometimes solid and handmodelled like the rest of the body, sometimes wheel-turned and hollow (Plate 14). This represents an ankle-length garment which was as traditional for men as for women across the Near East. Consequently, in the absence of any specific indications, attempts to relate it to the presumed tree-shaped or trunk-like symbol of Asherah lack both conviction and any direct justification. Indeed, where paint survives, it supports interpretation as a garment. The two most distinctive features of these females are their exaggerated breasts and the variation between handmodelled ('pinched') heads and mouldmade heads equipped with a peg of clay to be dowelled into the body.

The extreme exaggeration and fullness of the breasts, at times barely supported by the hands placed beneath them, and often in danger of toppling the figure forward, are a novelty. As the white-washed surface, with its painted details, is so often eroded off the figure or, if extant is damaged, it is not now clear whether the breasts were covered or exposed, as is the case on some female clay plaques elsewhere in the Levant (as described in the previous lecture). Whatever the case, the modern use of the epithet 'nurturing' is appropriate. It defines the contrast between them and the wholly nude, young females of the Canaanite clay plaques on the one hand and, on the other, the clearly pregnant Phoenician female terracottas. In Syria some of the local female pillar figurines hold a child in their arms (cf. Plate 12).

The variation between crudely pinched and moulded faces on the Judean Pillar Figurines is marked but still unexplained. The moulded faces have much in common with the so-called 'woman at the window' motif on Syro-Phoenician ivory carvings (cf. Weippert 1988: 631). As her identity remains no less uncertain than theirs, this comparison may serve only to strengthen the idea of an ultimate source in the north for this figurine type. Kletter (1996: 52) proposed that 'a cautious estimation of a few dozen moulds for all the Judean Pillar Figurines (known) is more than likely . . . we are dealing with mass production, of which only a small part has been discovered so far'. No such mould has yet been published.

The fine detail in some cases may indicate that they were cut in metal or stone.

No male image is known with a mouldmade face at this time. Later, in the Achaemenid Persian Empire, horsemen in Cyprus (cf. Young and Young 1955: 192) and in Syro-Phoenicia (cf. Elayi 1991) were given them. It has been suggested that they represent a famous hero or distinguished person with whom the donor of the votive image wished to associate himself. In the case of the Judean females, if regarded as votives, similar aspirations might apply; if seen as 'Asherahs', this feature might replicate in miniature the face of a major cult statue representing her (cf. Hadley 2000, 200–202).

The impact of the problem of 'Yahweh and (his) asherah' on the study of Iron Age terracottas in Judah has, by its exclusive concentration on the females as possible representations of this goddess, overshadowed the male figurines in the repertory. They are predominantly horse-riders (Plate 15). They are apparently less numerous, if no less widespread and recurrent than the females. Moreover, an unknown number of surviving horses may originally have carried riders.

Whereas the female pillar figurines are now commonly identified as 'Asherahs', there would appear to be a general reluctance to propose a divine identity for the males and no consensus when the attempt is made. Indeed, both Yahweh and such Canaanite gods as Baal and El have advocates. Keel and Uehlinger (1998: 345) are cautious: 'if the Palestinian riders ... belong to the sphere of that kind of El-like god of heaven and creator god, who would hardly have been anyone other than Yahweh in Judah, then the terracotta statuettes could possibly be understood as popular, anthropomorphic representations of the *"Host of Heaven"'*. Such proposals, however, raise the delicate question of how far it is reasonable to go in seeking to reconcile surviving material evidence with such Biblical information.

If these horseriders are assessed, however, as an aspect of the contemporary Near Eastern repertory of terracottas as a whole, they will be seen to be far from exceptional or isolated. Indeed, there was an unprecedented and widespread popularity of terracotta horsemen in the mature Iron Age in the Near East (cf. Moorey 2000). In Syria, where they appear together with female pillar figurines, both categories are usually described as human suppliants or toys, not as supernatural beings (cf. Woolley 1952, 257, pl.70; Moorey 1980, 100–102), as also in Cyprus (cf. Young and Young 1955) (Plate 13). In Transjordan Dornemann (1983: 137–8) remarked of the local terracotta horse-riders that 'it would be difficult ...

to see in our figurines anything other than representations of local people as cavalrymen' (cf. Prag 2001: 227). Indeed, the popularity amongst men of self-images as horsemen is likely to have been inspired by the new military role of cavalry in local and invading armies (cf. Lémaire 1998) and the social prestige conferred by identification with it on men of all ranks. *Ezekiel* (23: 23–4, cf. 6–7) points to 'all the Assyrians with them, young and desirable, all governors and nobles, all famous officers and horsemen . . .'. Josephus in *The Antiquities of the Jews* (XI.6.254) is more explicit still: 'If you wish to cover with glory the man whom you say you love let him ride on horseback wearing the same dress as yourself'. It has already been observed that when there is a male component amongst Near Eastern terracotta repertories in historic contexts it is at times of major socio-political change, as in third millennium Sumer and Syria. In the previous cases model chariots accompany the males as the appropriate, then new, form of transport in war.

In Judah terracotta horsemen range from carefully modelled and realistic images, though none have mouldmade heads, to very schematic males mounted on stylized horses. A still isolated example of an inscribed horse's head, from Samaria (Crowfoot *et al.* 1957: no.3, pl.13), bears a man's name, indicating that they might be 'owned' or 'dedicated' by individuals. Horses and horsemen are less exclusively concentrated in Judah than the pillar female figurines; but outside Judah they differ in technique and in the degree of plastic detail (cf. Gilbert-Peretz 1996: 38).

Much controversy has been stimulated by Kenyon's (1971: 120; 1974: 142) suggestion, relative to her finds in Cave I in Jerusalem, that the clay disks set between the ears of some of the terracotta horses are 'sun-disks' relating them to the 'horses of the sun' removed by King Josiah from the Temple in Jerusalem (II *Kings* 23:11). But these were, in fact, chariot not ridden horses. This phenomenon was not confined to terracotta horses from Jerusalem nor is it certain that these are not just rosettes or dressed forelocks, both standard ways of manipulating a horse's mane for decorative effect (cf. Holland 1977: 149–50). Consequently, for example, Ahlström's (1984: 22–3) argument that the horses with sun-disks represented 'Yahweh's horses', because Yahweh 'was associated with horses in his capacity as a solar deity' may be no more cogent than Kenyon's original proposal (Plate 15).

Disks are, in fact, rare amongst Judean horse figurines (cf. Kletter 1996: 13). There is a marked contrast between horse terracottas where the modeller has omitted details of the harnessing and those on which much attention has been paid to it. This, it should be noted, is more evident at present on sites not in Judah, notably at Hazor (Yadin 1960, fig. 103: 8–9; 1961, pl.177: 22, 216: 16).

If the male and female images are considered together, plausible arguments may be advanced for regarding both as votive figurines in human form rather than as anthropomorphic images of deities. There is, at present, no compelling argument in the case of the male-riders for a supernatural identity and only debatable ones for the females. Whatever the case, there is no evidence in the archaeological record for male and female pairs. These images from Israel and Judah, on present evidence, might well be set within the wider Near Eastern repertories of terracottas in the mature Iron Age, where such images are taken to represent members of the local communities as suppliants or votaries rather than deities. Until *both* male and female images may be convincingly accommodated amongst the deities of early Israelite religion, this is arguably the more probable identity for them. Indeed, there are grounds for proposing that both may have been supplicating the same deity, whether male or female. As was indicated in the previous lecture, the nude females of both the Egyptianizing and Syro-Mesopotamian tradition appear conspicuously amongst the apotropaic imagery on horse-harnessing. One of the most remarkable assemblages of terracotta male and female imagery from a Near Eastern site in the second quarter of the first millennium BC is that recovered from the Cypriot sanctuary of Apollo at Kourion (cf. Young and Young 1955), where the males are again riders. At many early shrines in the Greek World this god received offerings similar to those dedicated to female deities to the extent that some scholars have characterized him as *kourotrophos* ('nurturer': Voyatzis 1998: 146). If terracottas are to be seen as representing the deliverer not the receiver of prayers then the sex of the deity addressed is not necessarily evident.

It was indicated in the previous lecture that in Late Bronze Age Canaan the inadequacy of published information precluded the most basic statistics, not least for the occurrence of zoomorphic terracottas. They appear, however, to have been even more common than the anthropomorphic moulded images of nude females. In Holland's (1977) census of Iron Age terracottas in Israel and Judah zoomorphic images outnumber anthropomorphic by 3:2. Out of the 1300 terracottas subsequently published from Shiloh's Jerusalem excavations 926 were animals (cf. Gilbert-Peretz 1996), mainly quadrupeds. Horses, with or without riders, are conspicuous. In some areas of Kenyon's Jerusalem excavations the proportion of zoomorphic to anthropomorphic terracottas was as high as 6:1 (cf. Prag 2001). Many are too crudely modelled, as had always been the case, for identification. Naturalism would not generally appear to have been uppermost in the modeller's mind except with exotic forms—if the given identities are reliable. Amongst the animals and birds listed for Ophel are cattle, sheep, various horned species (deer; ibex; gazelle), a hyena, an elephant, a bear (?), hippopotami, a camel and an ostrich (cf. Tchernov 1996; Holland 1977).

Domestic ruminants were the major component of sacrifices in ancient Israel, whilst birds, especially doves and turtle doves, were also victims. Wild ungulates, especially deer and gazelle, feature amongst bones recovered from archaeological sites identified as cultic; but they are not mentioned in Old Testament prescriptions (cf. Borowski 1998: 227). If these zoomorphic terracottas were substitutes for sacrificial animals, such a role would not appear to account for them all.

It is no more easy, however, to establish a mythological significance for them, either individually or collectively. Animal names were certainly used for Canaanite and Israelite deities (cf. Miller 1970) and doves were traditionally associated with goddesses of love (cf. Ziffer 1998). Bull imagery was used for Baal, El and Yahweh; lion imagery for Asherah, Astarte and Anat, and for Yahweh; but whereas bulls are listed amongst published zoomorphic terracottas, lions do not seem to be. It is only through such generalized concepts of deities as 'Masters or Mistresses of Animals' that this variety of domestic and wild animals, together with birds, maybe embraced as symbols and then into a pantheon with roots deep in the Canaanite World. Keel and Uehlinger (1998, 277-8) have noted that on local seals at this time, though indigenous animal images (caprids, deer and lions) are still evident, they were now depicted without identifying gender and mother animals suckling their young were absent.

The rarest, and most unusual, of these miniature clay models are those representing furniture and very occasionally, as in Jerusalem Cave 1, buildings (Plate 16). Kletter (1996: 66) has listed 'at least' eleven female terracottas found together with models of beds, couches, chairs, benches or stools, and tables. Scattered examples are recurrent, some found in tombs. Such models are not known in the Late Bronze Age Canaanite terracotta repertory; but they do have precursors locally in the third millennium BC (Early Bronze Age) when they appear sporadically in the earliest urban settlements there (cf. Beck 1993; Miroschedji 1997). The most striking antecedents are the famous "Ashdoda" terracottas of Philistine culture with their striking fusion of a female image and a bed or throne (cf. Stager 1995, pl. on p.333). Terracotta model vehicles are all but unknown in Iron Age Israel and Judah (cf. Keel and Uehlinger 1998:

344). When comparable terracotta models of furniture and chariots (cf. Cholidis 1992; Stone 1993) had been manufactured in Babylonia a millennium earlier, they had borne divine symbols in some cases, as if representing furnishings in the "houses (temples) of the deities" but these are absent from the Judean examples. As with contemporary Phoenician terracottas these models represent ordinary household furnishings.

In a society and amongst people where furniture is likely to have been minimal, the attention given to it on occasion by modellers in Judah, even if only as a minor constituent of their repertory, is striking. Traditional interpretations, by highlighting the couches or seats as birthing aids, have emphasized nurturing and maternity in explanation of this model furniture; but this overlooks the tables and occasional model buildings. If the full range of male and female images, of animals and birds, and of furniture are taken together, they epitomize the primary pre-occupations of the common people, whether acting individually or corporately: the continuity of the family (past, present and future) and of the household in all its aspects. Which supernatural powers were particularly solicited through these images is not self-evident and not yet elucidated beyond reasonable doubt by any written evidence directly associated with them.

The domestic contexts, broadly defined, of these terracottas may be significant. At present, the archaeological record for Israel and Judah does not include small self-contained urban or rural shrines honouring local deities, like those already evident in Philistia (Ashdod), Phoenicia (Sarepta) and greater Edom, where votive terracottas were placed with other offerings in the presence of a deity statue or monumental symbol (cf. Hachlili 1971; Pritchard 1978; Cohen and Yisrael 1995).

For present purposes a single example may be cited: the isolated rural shrine, built in the seventh century BC, on a hill top at Horvat Qitmit, south-southeast of modern Beersheva, at a time when Edomites may have controlled this region. Its contents, as excavated, have justly been described as 'the most outstanding assemblage of Late Iron Age cultic statuary and figurines found to date in Israel or Palestine' (Keel and Uehlinger 1998: IX). Another such shrine was subsequently excavated at _En Hazeva in the Arava (Cohen and Yisrael 1995). In both shrines the anthropomorphic terracottas represent worshippers not deities, suppliants to Qos, the regional god of Edom. Whilst 'En Hazeva has a homogeneous assemblage, that at Horvat Qitmit is more interregional, reflecting how throughout the Late Bronze and Iron Ages the iconography of cultic imagery in the Levant was '"eclectic" in nature' (Beck 1996, 112). At Horvat Qitmit the exception amongst anthropomorphic forms is a hollow, wheel made and freely modelled male head with three horns set round a conical knob of hair on the top of the head. These features indicate a deity whose sex may be established by contrast with the complete female figurines in the shrine (cf. Beck 1995, no.68, pp.120–1).

One of the very rare parallels for this head is to be found on a miniature bronze statue of a goddess, with exactly the same triple horns, found early in the last century at Kafr Kanna in Galilee. She stands on a podium supported by four nude females at each corner, illustrating the lesser status of such figures (cf. Beck 1995, fig.3: 57b). They endorse the view, argued in the previous lecture, that the nude female, without attributes indicative of a divinity, represents a servant or acolyte of a goddess, not the goddess herself.

At Horvat Qitmit all the solid clay female figurines were mouldmade in the Canaanite-Phoenician tradition. At least two, nude and clasping their breasts, without any distinctive headdress, are parts of pairs formerly flanking the entrance to model shrines (Beck 1995: nos. 107–8, p.101; fig.3: 66–9). Such model shrines, already described in the previous lecture, without anthropomorphic decoration, are also represented amongst the finds at Horvat Qitmit (Beck 1995: nos. 206–10, p.173, figs. 3:119a,b). The terracotta animals there were modelled with solid or wheel-turned hollow bodies. Bovids, ibexes and dogs, with possible horses and lions, some rather sphinx-like, may be recognized amongst them (cf. Beck 1995: 140–1). The clay birds include cocks and ostriches, which would then have been common locally. This shrine, although culturally distinct from those that may have existed in Israel and Judah, illustrates how the primary elements in assemblages cross all cultural boundaries at this time, though they vary in style.

The most evident, and consequently the most discussed, potential clue to the function of the varied terracottas of Judah, particularly outside mortuary contexts, is the fact that such a high percentage overall are found broken in some way. For over a century scholars have postulated deliberate rather than accidental breakage as it is so common and would at times appear to be patterned. Thick body parts were consistently broken; at others heads were neatly cut off the neck of female figurines. After a series of experiments of his own making and breaking female figurines, Kletter (1996: 54–6) decided that 'accidental breakage was the better explanation'; but his own meticulous documentation of ancient broken Judean Pillar Figurines (Kletter 1996, fig.25) tends rather to the opposite conclusion, as does the body of evidence from Jerusalem (Ophel) and Samaria E-207 already discussed here.

Amongst those for whom breakage, at least in certain cases, was deliberate, two explanations are current: either they were broken by religious reformers seeking to eliminate popular cults, notably that of Asherah, anathematized by state religious authorities (cf. Dever 1991; 2001, 193–198) *or* they were routinely destroyed by those who made them, after they had served their purpose, to eliminate magical powers with which they had been endowed to be effective (cf. Franken 1995). In view of the fact that the use of these figurines extended from at least the eighth to the early sixth century BC intermittent iconoclasm seems improbable as a general explanation for breakage. It may be significant that a large percentage of Iron Age mouldmade relief plaques have survived complete outside tombs in Israel and elsewhere in the Levant where they remained in use, though absent from Judah. This is another trait distinguishing them from the handmodelled, free-standing anthropomorphic terracottas popular in Judah, perhaps endorsing the conclusion, already mentioned, that in daily life the plaques had served as personal talismans.

If the functions and identities of terracottas in Israel and Judah before the Exile remain obscure, their disappearance is more evident. The Judean terracotta repertory did not survive the Exile in Babylonia. After many excavations and surveys in Judea, and to a rather lesser extent in Samaria, there is still a marked absence of terracotta figurines from areas known to have been occupied by returning Jewish exiles (cf. Stern 1989; 2001). By contrast, in Idumea, Philistia, Phoenicia and Galilee, particularly along the Mediterranean coast, there are many rubbish pits associated with shrines full of discarded terracottas and stone figurines dating to the time of the Achaemenid Persian Empire. They, however, reflect traditions largely distinct from those examined in this lecture.

5. Closing comments

These lectures have been permeated by ambiguities and by consequent problems of validation. They have perhaps illustrated all too well my general view that this is a subject where too much certainty may have prematurely entered in, not least at the popular interface of archaeology and biblical studies. It may have been possible to strengthen the invalidation of some hypotheses; but rarely to offer confident confirmation of others. At the best of times few things in archaeology are more elusive than the definition of functions determined socially rather than inherent in the objects themselves. Potentially, a single type or form may have served a variety of purposes dependent on the social contexts of its use. This is more rather than less likely with low status artefacts like terracottas, since they would have circulated and been disposed of in a wider variety of contexts than images of precious materials made by expert craftsmen for an *élite*. It is no surprise then that open questions and potential multiplicities of function and identity should still be more appropriate than confident answers and fixed roles in any approach to the miniature clay images of Canaan, Israel and Judah. That is why they present a continuing challenge.

PLATE 13

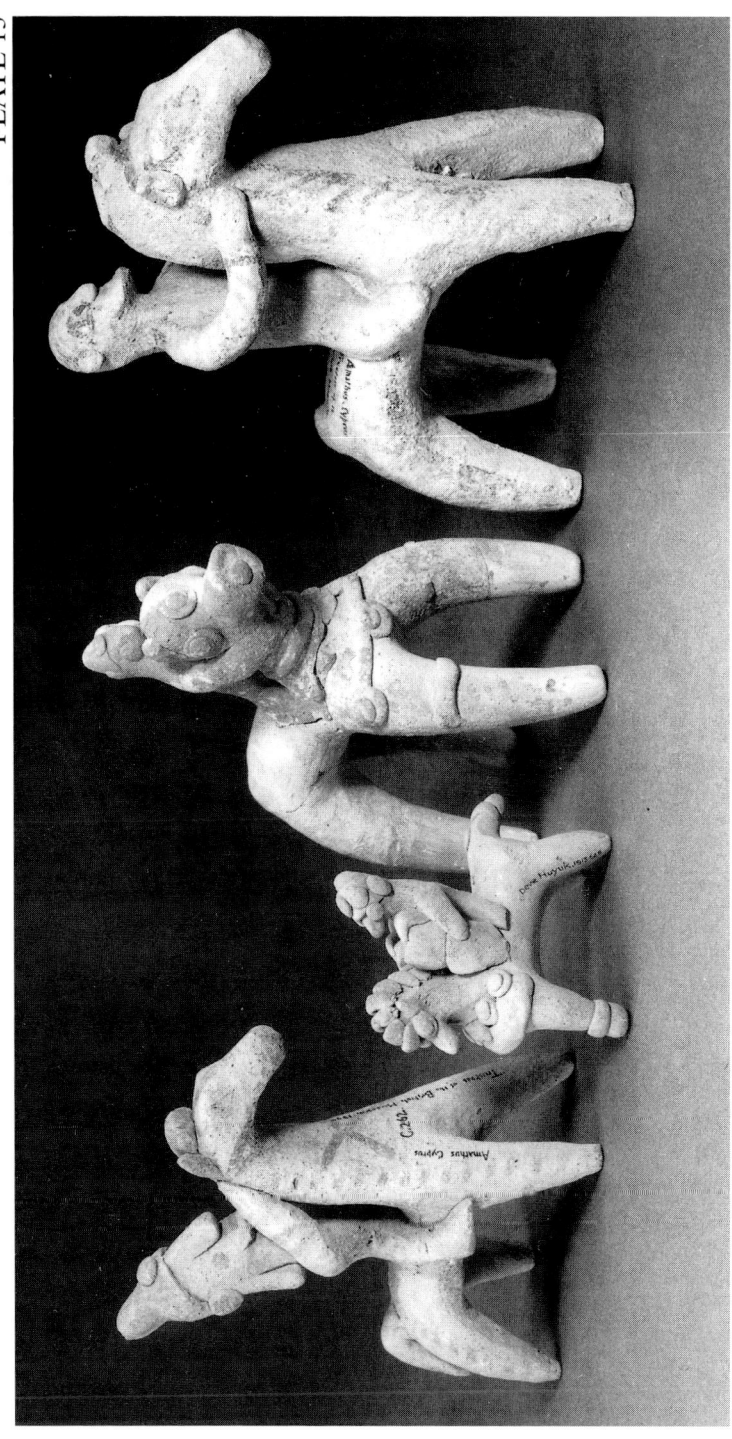

Handmade terracotta horsemen figurines; from sites in Syria (centre) and Amathus in Cyprus (sides); seventh to fifth centuries BC; 12.4 cm; 14.2 cm; 12.2 cm; 13.5 cm high (C.262; 1913.648; 1914.872; C.261).

PLATE 14

Terracotta Judean female pillar-figurine; said to be from a tomb at Bethlehem; seventh century BC; 17.5 cm high (British Museum 93091).

PLATE 15

Terracotta horse and rider (note the extent of damage); excavated from Cave I at Jerusalem (Ophel); seventh century BC; 10.5 cm high (horse); 5.4 cm high (man) (1968.1384; 1968.1386).

PLATE 16

Terracotta model of a building (note extent of damage); excavated from Cave I at Jerusalem (Ophel); seventh century BC; 8.8 3 7 cm (1968.1404).

Abbreviations

AASOR	*The Annual of the American Schools of Oriental Research* (New Haven, Connecticut).
ADAJ	*Annual of the Department of Antiquities, Jordan* (Amman).
AJA	*American Journal of Archaeology* (Cambridge, Mass.).
AO	*Altorientalische Forschungen* (Berlin).
BAR	*Biblical Archaeology Review* (Washington).
BASOR	*Bulletin of the American Schools of Oriental Research* (Jerusalem and Baghdad).
CAJ	*Cambridge Archaeological Journal* (Cambridge, U.K.).
IA	*Iranica Antiqua* (Leiden).
IEJ	*Israel Exploration Journal* (Jerusalem).
JCS	*Journal of Cuneiform Studies* (New Haven, Connecticut).
JEOL	*Jaarbericht 'Ex Oriente Lux'* (Leiden).
JNES	*Journal of Near Eastern Studies* (Chicago).
OAJ	*Oxford Art Journal* (Oxford).
OIC	*Oriental Institute (Chicago University) Communications*.
OJA	*Oxford Journal of Archaeology* (Oxford).
RB	*Revue Biblique* (Jerusalem).
RlA	*Reallexikon der Assyriologie und vorderasiatische Archäologie* (Berlin).
UF	*Ugarit Forschungen* (Münster).
ZAW	*Zeitschrift für die alttestamentlichen Wissenschaft* (Berlin: New York).
ZDP-V	*Zeitschrift des Deutschen Palästina-Vereins* (Wiesbaden).

Bibliography

Abusch, T. & van der Toorn, K. (1999), *Mesopotamian Magic: Textual, Historical and Interpretative Perspectives* (Groningen).

Ahlström, G.W. (1984), 'An Archaeological Picture of Iron Age Religions in Ancient Palestine', *Studia Orientalia* 55(3): 117–145.

Akkermans, P. M. M. G. & Verhoeven, M. (1995), 'A image of complexity: the burnt village at Late Neolithic Sabi Abyad, Syria', *AJA* 90: 5–32.

Albright, W. F. (1943), *The Excavation of Tell Beit Mirsim III: The Iron Age* (*AASOR* 21–22 (1941–1943), New Haven, Connecticut).

Amiet, P. (1995), 'La naissance des dieux: approche iconographique, *RB* 102: 485–505.

Auerbach, E. (1994), *Terracotta Plaques from the Diyala and their Archaeological and Cultural Contexts* (The University of Chicago: UMI Dissertation Services).

Bachelot, L. (1990), 'Le bassin aux femmes' in J-M Durand (ed.), *Tell Mohammad Diyab: Campagnes de 1987 et 1988* (Paris), 47–50.

Badre, L. (1980), *Les figurines anthropomorphes en terre cuite á l'Âge du Bronze en Syrie* (Paris).

Bahrani, Z. (1996), 'The Hellenization of Ishtar: nudity, fetishism, and the production of cultural differentiation in ancient art', *OAJ* 19(2): 3–16.

Barag, D. (1970), 'Mesopotamian Core-Formed Glass Vessels (1500–500 BC),' in A. L. Oppenheim *et al. Glass and Glassmaking in Ancient Mesopotamia* (Corning), 129–199.

Beck, P. (1990), 'The Cult-Stands from Taanach: Aspects of the Iconographic Tradition of Early Iron Age Cult Objects in Palestine', in I. Finkelstein and N. Na'aman (eds.), *From Nomadism to Monarchy: Archaeological and Historical Aspects of Early Israel* (Jerusalem), 352–381.

—— (1993), 'Early Bronze Age "bed-models" reconsidered,' *Tel Aviv* 20: 33–40.

—— (1995), 'Catalogue of Cult Objects and Study of the Iconography,' in I. Beit-Arieh (ed.) *Horvat Qitmit: an Edomite Shrine in the Biblical Negev* (Tel Aviv University), 27–208.

—— (1996), 'Horvat Qitmit Revisited via 'En Hazeva,' *Tel Aviv* 23: 102–114.

—— (1999), 'Human figure with tambourine,' in I. Beit-Arieh (ed.), *Tel 'Ira: a Stronghold in the Biblical Negev* (Tel Aviv), 386–94.

Beit-Arieh, I. (1995), *Horvat Qitmit: an Edomite Shrine in the Biblical Negev* (Tel Aviv University).

Bienert, H-D. (1990), 'The Er-Ram Stone Mask at the Palestine Exploration Fund, London', *OJA* 9: 257–261.

—— (1991), 'Skull Cult in Prehistoric Near East,' *Journal of Prehistoric Religion* 5: 9–23.
Biggs, R.D. (1967), *ŠA.ZI.GA: Ancient Mesopotamian Potency Incantations* (New York).
Biran, A. (1994), *Biblical Dan* (Jerusalem).
Black, J. & Green, A. (1992), *Gods, Demons and Symbols of ancient Mesopotamia: an illustrated dictionary* (British Museum, London).
Borowski, O. (1998), *Every Living Thing: Daily Use of Animals in Ancient Israel* (Walnut Creek: London: New York).
Braudel, F. (1980), *On History* (London).
Bretschneider, J. (1991), *Architekturmodelle in Vorderasien und in östlichen Agaïs vom Neolithikum bis in das I Jahrtausend* (Kevelaer and Neukirchen-Vluyn).
—— (1991a), 'Götter in Schreinen....', *UF* 23, 13–32.
Brusasco, P. (1999–2000), 'Family archives and the social use of space in Old Babylonian Houses at Ur,' *Mesopotamia* XXXIV-V: 5–173.
Bunomovitz, S. (1995), 'On the edge of Empires—Late Bronze Age (1500–1200 BCE),' in T. E. Levy (ed.) *The Archaeology of Society in the Holy Land* (Leicester University Press, London), 321–331.
Cauvin, J. (2000), *The Birth of the Gods and the Origins of Agriculture* (Cambridge).
Cholidis, N. (1992), *Möbel in Ton: Untersuchungen zur archäologischen und religions-geschichtlichen Bedeutung der Terrakottamodelle von Tischen, Stühlen, und Betten aus dem Alten Orient* (Münster).
Cohen, R. & Yisrael, Y. (1995), *On the Road to Edom: Discoveries from 'En Hazeva* (Israel Museum, Jerusalem).
Collingwood, R. G. (1939), *An Autobiography* (Oxford).
Collon, D. (1986), *Western Asiatic Seals in the British Museum: Cylinder Seals III: Isin Larsa to Old Babylonian Periods* (London).
—— (1995), *Ancient Near Eastern Art* (British Museum, London).
Crowfoot, J. W. et al. (1942), *Samaria-Sebaste I: The Buildings* (London).
—— (1957), *Samaria-Sebaste III: the Objects* (London).
Culican, W. (1976), 'A Terracotta Shrine from Achzib,' *ZDP-V* 92, 47–59.
Dales, G. F. (1960), *Mesopotamian and Related Female Figurines. Their Chronology, Diffusion and Cultural Function* (University of Pennsylvania; UMI Dissertation Services).
D'Amore, P. (1998), 'La Coroplastica di Tell Afis,' in S. Mazzoni (ed.) *Tell Afis et l'Età de Ferro*) (Pisa), 75–98.
Day, J. (2000), *Yahweh and the Gods and Goddesses of Canaan* (Sheffield).
De Meyer, L. (1978), *Tell ed-Der* II (Leuven).
Dever, W. G. (1991), 'Women's Popular Religion, suppressed in the Bible. Now revealed by archaeology,' *BAR* 17(2): 64–5.
—— (1996) 'Archaeology and the Religions of Israel: a review article', *BASOR* 301: 83–90.
—— (1999), 'How Khirbet el Qôm and Kuntillet 'Ajrud have changed the picture', *Eretz Israel* 26: 9*-15*.

Dever, W. G. (2001), *What did the Biblical Writers know and when did they know it?* (Grand Rapids, Michigan and Cambridge).

Dikaios, P. (1938), 'The Excavations at Vounous—Bellapais in Cyprus 1931–2,' *Archaeologia* 88: 1–174.

Dornemann, R. H. (1983), *The Archaeology of the Transjordan in the Bronze and Iron Age* (Milwaukee Public Museum).

Driver, G. R. (1948), *Semitic Writing* (London).

Elayi, J. (1991), 'Deux "ateliers" de coroplastes nord-phéniciens et nord-syriens sous l'empire perse', *IA* XXVI: 181–216.

Eshel, I. & Prag, K. (1995), *Excavations by K. M. Kenyon in Jerusalem 1961–1967* (British School of Archaeology in Jerusalem; Oxford).

Finkelstein, I. (1995), 'The great transformation: the "Conquest" of the highlands frontiers and the rise of the territorial states,' in T. E. Levy (ed.), 349–365.

Foster, B. (1974), 'Wisdom and the Gods in Ancient Mesopotamia', *Orientalia* NS. 43: 344–354.

Fowler, M. D. (1985), 'Excavated Figurines: A Case for Identifying a Site as Sacred?,' *ZAW* 97: 333–344.

Franken, H. J. (1995), 'Cave I at Jerusalem—an interpretation', in S. Bourke and J-P Descoeudres (ed.), *Trade, Contact, and the Movement of Peoples in the Eastern Mediterranean: Studies in Honour of J. Basil Hennessy* (Sydney), 233–240.

Franken, H. J. & Steiner, M. L. (1990), *Excavations in Jerusalem 1961–1967, II: The Iron Age Extramural Quarter on the South-East Hill* (British School of Archaeology in Jerusalem; Oxford).

Frankfort, H. (1936), 'Progress of the Work of the Oriental Institute in Iraq, 1934–35', *OIC*, no.20 (Chicago).

Garfinkel, Y. (1994), 'Ritual burial of cultic objects: the earliest evidence', *CAJ* 4: 159–188.

Ghirshman, R. (1976), *Terrasses Sacrées de Bard-è Néchandeh et Misjid-i Solaiman* (*MDAI* XLV; Paris).

Gilbert-Peretz, D. (1996), 'Ceramic Figurines', in *Excavations in the City of David 1978–1985*. D.T. & A. de Groot (eds.); *Qedem* 35 (Jerusalem), 29–134.

Goelet, O. (1993), 'Nudity in Ancient Egypt', *Source* XII (2): 20–31.

Gombrich, E. H. (1993), *A Lifelong Interest. Conversations in Art and Science with Didier Eribon* (London).

Goodison, L. & Morris, C. (ed.) (1998), *Ancient Goddesses: The Myths and the Evidence* (British Museum, London).

Gossman, L. (2000), *Basel in the Age of Burckhardt: A Study in Unseasonable Ideas* (Chicago).

Grayson, A. K. (1991), *The Royal Inscriptions of Mesopotamia: Assyrian Periods 2: Assyrian Rulers of the Early First Millennium B.C. I* (1114–859 BC) (Toronto).

Green, A. R. (1983), 'Neo-Assyrian apotropaic figures: figurines, rituals, and monumental art...', *Iraq* 45: 87–96.

Grissom, C. A. (2000), 'Neolithic Statues from 'Ain Ghazal: Construction and Form', *AJA* 104: 25–45.

Gubel, E. (1986), 'Coroplastic', in *Les Phéniciens et le monde mediterranéen* (exhibition catalogue; Brussels), 112–141.
Hachlili, R. (1971), 'Figurines and kernoi (Areas d, Hand Trench C1', in M. Dothan *et al.*, *Ashdod II-III: the Second and Third Seasons of Excavations 1963, 1965; Soundings 1967 ('Atiquot* IX-X; Jerusalem), 125–135.
Hadley, J. M. (2000), *The Cult of Asherah in Ancient Israel and Judah* (Cambridge).
Hestrin, R. (1987), 'Lachish Ewer and the 'Asherah', *IEJ* 37: 212–223.
Holladay, J. S., Jr. (1987), 'Religion in Israel and Judah under the Monarchy: an explicitly archaeological approach', in Miller, P. D. *et al.*, *Ancient Israelite Religion: Essays in Honor of F. M. Cross* (Philadelphia), 249–299.
—— (1995), 'The Kingdoms of Israel and Judah: Political and Economic Centralization in the Iron IIA-B (ca. 1000–750 BC)', in T. E. Levy (ed.) 1995, 368–398.
Holland, T. (1977), 'A Study of Palestinian Iron Age Baked Clay Figurines, with special reference to Jerusalem: Cave 1', *Levant* 9: 121–155.
Huizinga, J. (1949), *Homo Ludens: A Study of the Play-element in Culture* (London).
Jacob-Rost, L. & Freydank, H. (1981), 'Eine altassyrische Votivinschrift', *AO* 8: 325–327.
Jacobsen, Th. (1987), 'Pictures and Pictorial Language (the Burney Relief)', in M. Mindlin *et al.* (eds.) *Figurative Language in the Ancient Near East* (School of Oriental and African Studies, London University), 1–11.
Kantor, H. J. (1962), 'A Bronze Plaque with Relief Decoration from Tell Tainat', *JNES* 21:93–117.
Keel, O. & Uehlinger, C. (1998), *Gods, Goddesses and Images of God in Ancient Israel* (Edinburgh).
Kenyon, K. M. (1956), *Digging Up Jericho* (London).
—— (1967), *Jerusalem, Excavating 3000 Years of History* (London).
—— (1971), *Royal Cities of the Old Testament* (London).
—— (1974), *Digging up Jerusalem* (London).
Kletter, R. (1996), *The Judean Pillar-Figurines and the Archaeology of Asherah* (BAR International Series 636; Oxford).
Kyrieleis, H. & Röllig, W. (1988), 'Ein altorientalischer Pferdeschmuck aus dem Heraion von Samos', *Mitteilungen des Deutschen Archäologischen Instituts, athenische Abteilung* 103, 37–75.
Lambert, W. G. (1998), 'Technical terminology for Creation in the Ancient Near East,' in *Intellectual Life in the Ancient Near East* (Proceedings of the 43rd Rencontre Assyriologique, Prague), 189–193.
Lapp, P. W. (1964) 'The 1963 Excavations at Tell Ta'annek', *BASOR* 173: 39–41.
—— (1967), 'The 1966 Excavations at Tell Ta'annek', *BASOR* 185: 2–39.
—— (1969), 'The 1968 Excavations at Tell Ta'annek', *BASOR* 195: 42–45.
Lémaire, A. (1998), 'Chars et cavaliers dans l'ancien Israel', *Transeuphratène* 15: 165–182.

Levi-Strauss, C. (1966), *The Savage Mind* (London).
Levy, T. E. (ed.) (1995), *The Archaeology of Society in the Holy Land* (London).
Lipinski, E. (1986), 'The Syro-Palestinian Iconography of Women and Goddesses', *IEJ* 36:87–98.
McAdam, E. (1993), 'Clay Figurines', in A. Green (ed.), *Abu Salbikh Excavations 4: The 6GAsh-Tip and its contents: cultic or administrative discard from the temple?* (British School of Archaeology in Iraq; London), 83–109.
—— (1997), 'The figurines from the 1982–5 seasons of excavations at 'Ain Ghazal', *Levant* 29: 115–145.
McGovern, P. E. (1985), *Late Bronze Palestinian Pendants: Innovation in a Cosmopolitan Age* (Sheffield).
Magrill, P. & Middleton, A. (2001), 'Did the Potter's Wheel go out of use in Late Bronze Age Palestine?' *Antiquity* 75: 137–144.
Marchetti, N. (2000) 'Clay Figurines of the Middle Bronze Age from Northern Inner Syria: Chronology, Symbolic Meaning and Historical Relations', in P. Matthiae *et al.* (eds.) 2000, 839–867.
Marchetti, N. & Nigro, L. (1997), 'Cultic activities in the sacred area of Ishtar at Ebla during the Old Syrian Period: the *Favissae* F.5327 and F.5238', *JCS* 49: 1–44.
Matthiae, P. *et al.* (eds.) (2000) *Proceedings of the First International Congress of the Archaeology of the Ancient Near East: Rome, May 18th – 23rd 1998* I (Rome).
Mazar, A. (1985), 'Pottery plaques depicting Goddesses standing in Temple Facades', *Michmanim* 2: 5–18.
Mazar, A. & Camp, J. (2000), 'Will Tell Rehov save the United Monarchy?', *BAR* 26(2):38–51, 75.
Mazar, E. & Mazar, B. (1989), *Excavations in the South of the Temple Mount: The Ophel of Biblical Jerusalem* (Qedem 29; Jerusalem).
Mecquenem, R. de (*et al.*) (1943), *Mission Susiane: Archéologie susienne* (Paris).
Mellaart, J. (1967), *Çatal Hüyük: a Neolithic Town in Anatolia* (London).
Meshel, Z. (1978), *Kuntillet 'Ajrud: A Religious Centre from the Time of the Judaean Monarchy on the Border of Sinai* (Israel Museum, Jerusalem).
—— (1979), 'Did Yahweh have a consort?', *BAR* 5(2): 24–35.
Meskell, L. (1998), 'Intimate archaeologies the case of Kha and Merit', *World Archaeology* 29: 363–379.
Meyer, L.de (1978), *Tell ed-Der* II (Leuven).
Miller, P.D. (1970), 'Animal names as designations in Ugaritic and Hebrew', *UF* 2: 177–186.
Miroschedji, P. de (1997), 'La glyptique palestinienne du Bronze ancien' in A. Caubet (ed.), *De Chypre à la Bactriane, les sceaux du Proche-Orient ancien* (Paris).
Moon, J. (1987), *Abu Salbikh Excavations 3: Catalogue of Early Dynastic Pottery* (British School of Archaeology in Iraq, London).
Moorey, P. R. S. (1970), 'Cemetery at Kish: Grave Groups and Chronology', *Iraq* 32: 86–128.
—— (1978), *Kish Excavations 1923–1933* (Oxford).

Moorey, P. R. S. (1980), *Cemeteries of the First Millennium B.C. at Deve Hüyük, near Carchemish, salvaged by T. E. Lawrence and C. L. Woolley in 1913* (BAR International Series 87, Oxford).
—— (2000), 'Iran and the West: the Case of the "Persian" Riders in the Achaemenid Empire' R. Dittmann *et al.* (eds.) *Variatio Delectat Iran und Westen* (Münster), 469– 486.
—— (2002) 'Novelty and Tradition in Achaemenid Syria: the case of the clay "Astarte Plaques"' *IA* 37: 203–218.
Moorey, P. R. S. & Fleming, S. (1984), 'Problems in the study of the Anthropomorphic Metal Statuary from Syro-Palestine before 330 BC', *Levant* 16: 67–90.
Morris, D. (1985), *The Art of Ancient Cyprus* (London).
Morsch, M. G. F. (1998), 'Die Tonobjekte von Nevali Cori: neue Perspektiven in der figürlichen Plastik des akeramischen Neolithikums' in *Préhistoire d'Anatolie: Genèse de deux mondes* (Liège), 680.
Myres, J. L. (1923), 'Neolithic and Bronze Age cultures', in J. B. Bury *et al.* (ed.), *The Cambridge Ancient History* I: 57–110 (Cambridge).
Nakhai, B. A. (1994), 'What's a Bamah? How Sacred Space functioned in Ancient Israel', *BAR* 20(3): 18–30, 77–79.
Negbi, O. (1970), *The Hoards of Goldwork from Tell el-'Ajjul* (Göteborg).
Nishiyama, S. & Yoshizawa, S. (1997), 'Who worshipped the clay goddess?: the late first millennium BC terracotta figurines from Tell Mastuma, Northwest Syria', *Bulletin of the Ancient Orient Museum* (Tokyo), 17: 73–98.
Nováká, N. (1971), *Terres cuites de Tell Erfad* (Prague: Musée Nrstek).
Opificius, R. (1961), *Das altbabylonische Terrakotta-relief* (Berlin),
—— (1998), 'Eine Ischtardarstellung aus Tell Dscharablus-Tachtani', *Subartu* IV (2): 279–320.
Oppenheim, A. L. (1977), *Ancient Mesopotamia: Portrait of a Dead Civilization* (Revised edition; Chicago).
Orchard, J. J. (1967), *Ivories from Nimrud* I(2), *Equestrian Bridle-Harness Ornaments* (London).
Ottoson, M. (1980), *Temples and Cult Places in Palestine* (Uppsala).
Parrot, A. (1968), *Mission archéologique de Mari IV: Le 'Trésor' de Mari* (Paris).
Patai, R. (1967), *The Hebrew Goddess* (New York).
Peltenburg, E. J. (1994), 'Constructing authority—The Vounous enclosure model', *Opuscula Atheniensia* XX: 157–162.
—— (2000), 'From Nucleation to Dispersal. Late third millennium BC settlement patterns in the Near East and Aegean', *Subartu VII: La Djéziré et l'Euphrate syrien de la protohistoire à la fin du second millénaire av. J-C.* (Turnhout), 183–206.
Pinch, G. (1983), 'Childbirth and Female Figurines at Deir el-Medina and el-'Amarna', *Orientalia* 52: 405–414.
—— (1993), *Votive Offerings to Hathor* (Griffith Institute, Ashmolean Museum, Oxford).
Postgate, J. N. (1994), 'Text and figure in ancient Mesopotamia: match and mismatch', in Renfrew, C. & Zubrow, E. B. W. (eds.), *The Ancient Mind: Elements of Cognitive Archaeology* (Cambridge), 176–184.

Potts, T. F. *et al.* (1985), 'Preliminary Report on a Sixth Season of Excavation by the University of Sydney at Pella in Jordan 1983/84', *ADAJ* 29: 181–210.
Prag, K. (2001), 'Figurines, Figures and Contexts in Jerusalem and Regions to the East in the Seventh and Sixth Centuries B.C.', in A. Mazar (ed.), *Studies in the Archaeology of the Iron Age in Israel and Jordan* (J.S.O.T. Supplement Series 331; Sheffield), 217–234.
Prigneaud, J. (1978), 'Scribes et Graveurs à Jerusalem vers 700 av. J-C.', in P. R. S. Moorey & P. J. Parr (eds.), *Archaeology in the Levant... Kathleen Kenyon* (Warminster) 136–148.
Pritchard, J. B. (1943), *Palestinian Figurines in Relation to Certain Goddesses Known Through Literature* (New Haven, Conn.).
—— (1978), *Recovering Sarepta: A Phoenician City* (Princeton).
Pruss, A. & Novak, M. (2000), 'Terrakotten und Beinidole in sepulkralen Kontexten', *AO* 27: 184–195.
Quirke, S. (1998), 'Figures of clay: toys or ritual objects', in S. Quirke (ed.), *Lahun Studies* (SIA Publishing, Reigate, Surrey) 141–151.
Rapp, R. (1977), 'Gender and class: an archaeology of knowledge concerning the origin of the state', *Dialectical Archaeology* 2: 309–316.
Reiner, E. (1987), 'Magic Figurines, Amulets and Talismans', in A. Farkas (ed.), *Monsters and Demons in the Ancient and Medieval Worlds* (Mainz am Rhein), 27–36.
—— (1995), *Astral Magic in Mesopotamia* (The American Philosophical Society, Philadelphia).
Reyes, A. T. (1994), *Archaic Cyprus: A Study of the Textual and Archaeological Evidence* (Oxford).
Rollefson, G. (2000), 'Ritual and social structure in Neolithic Ain Ghazal', in I. Kuijt, (ed.), *Life in Neolithic Farming Communities: Social Organization, Identity and Differentiation* (London), 163–190.
Schmandt-Besserat, D. (1977), *Before Writing: From Counting to Cuneiform*, vol. 2: *Catalogue of Near Eastern Tokens* (Austin).
Schmitt, R. (1999), 'Philistäische Terrakottafiguren', *UF* 31: 577–676.
Schulman, A. R. (1981), 'Reshef times two', in W. K. Simpson & W. M. Davies (eds.), *Studies in Ancient Egypt, the Aegean and the Sudan: Essays in Honor of Dows Dunham* (Museum of Fine Arts, Boston), 157–166.
Serhal, C. D. (1995), *Terres Cuites Orientales: La Collection Klat* (London).
Stager, L. (1991), 'When Canaanites and Philistines ruled Ashkelon' *BAR* XVII (2): 24–43.
—— (1995), 'The Impact of the Sea Peoples in Canaan (1185–1050 BCE)'. in T. E. Levy (ed.) 1995, 332–348.
Steinkeller, P. (1999), 'On rulers, priests and sacred marriage: tracing the evolution of early Sumerian kingship', in K. Watanabe (ed.), *Priests and Officials in the Ancient Near East* (Tokyo), 103–137.
Stern, E. (1989), 'What happened to the Cult Figurines? Israelite Religion after the Exile', *BAR* 15(4): 22–9, 53–4.

—— (2001), 'Pagan Yahwism: the Folk Religion of Ancient Israel', *BAR* 27(3): 21–29.
Stone, E. (1993), 'Chariots of the Gods in Old Babylonian Mesopotamia (c. 2000–1600 BC)', *CAJ* 3: 83–107.
Tadmor, M. (1982), 'Female Cult Figurines in Late Canaan and Early Israel: Archaeological Evidence' in Ishida, T. (ed.), 'Studies in the Period of David and Solomon and Other Essays' (Tokyo and Winona Lake), 139–173.
Tappy, R. (1998), Review of Kletter 1996, *BASOR* 310: 85–9.
Tchernov, E. (1996), 'The Faunal World of the City of David as represented by the figurines', *Qedem* 35: 85–6.
Thomas, K. (1997), *Religion and the Decline of Magic. Studies in Popular Beliefs in sixteenth and seventeenth century England* (London).
Tringham, R. & Conkey, M. (1998), 'Rethinking figurines: a critical view from archaeology of Gimbutas, the "Goddess" and popular culture', in L.Goodison & C. Morris (eds.), 22–45.
Tufnell, O. (1958), *Lachish IV (Tell ed Duweir) The Bronze Age* (London).
Ucko, P. J. (1962), 'The Interpretation of Prehistoric Anthropomorphic Figurines', *Journal of the Royal Anthropological Institute* 92: 38–54.
—— (1968), *Anthropomorphic Figurines of Predynastic Egypt and Neolithic Crete* (Royal Anthropological Institute, London).
—— (1996) 'Mother, are you there?' *CAJ* 6: 300–304.
Van der Toorn, K. (1986) Review of U. Winter, *Frau und Göttin*' (1983) in *Bibliotheca Orientalis* 43: 493–499.
—— (1998), 'Goddesses in Early Israelite Religion', in L. Goodison & C. Morris (eds.), *Ancient Goddesses: The Myths and the Evidence* (British Museum, London), 83–97.
Van de Mieroop, M. (1997), *The Ancient Mesopotamian City* (Oxford).
Voigt, M. (1983), *Hajji Firuz Tepe, Iran: The Neolithic Settlement* (University Museum, Philadelphia).
—— (2000), 'Çatal Höyük in context: ritual at Early Neolithic sites in Central and Eastern Turkey', in I. Kuijt (ed.), *Life in Neolithic Farming Communities: Social Organization, Identity and Differentiation* (London), 163–190.
Voyatzis, M. E. (1998), 'From Athena to Zeus: an A-Z Guide to the Origins of Greek Goddesses', in L. Goodison & C. Morris (eds.), 133–147.
Walker, C. J. & Dick, M. B. (1999), 'The Mesopotamian *mīs pî* Ritual' in Dick, M. B., *Born in Heaven, Made on Earth: The Making of the Cult Image in the ancient Near East* (Eisenbraun, Winona Lake), 55–121.
Watelin, L. Ch. (1934), *Excavations at Kish (1925–30)* IV (Paris).
Weippert, H. (1988), *Palästina in vorhellenistischer Zeit* (Handbuch der Archäologie Vorderasien II/1; Münich).
Wengrow, D. (1998), '"The changing face of clay": continuity and change in the transition from village to urban life in the Near East', *Antiquity* 72: 783–795.
Westenholz, J. (1998), '*Goddesses of the Ancient Near East 3000–1000 BC*', in Goodison, L. & Morris, C. (eds.), *Ancient Goddesses: The Myths and the Evidence* (British Museum, London), 63–81.

Wicke, D. (1999), 'Altorientalische Pferdescheulappen', *UF* 31: 803–52.
Wiggermann, F. A. M. (1985–6), 'The staff of Ninsubura', *JEOL* 29: 3–34.
—— (1986), *Babylonian Prophylactic Figures: The Ritual Texts* (Amsterdam).
—— (1992) *Mesopotamian Protective Spirits: The Ritual Texts* (Groningen).
—— (1998) 'Nackte Göttin', *RlA* 9: 46–64.
Winter, U. (1983), *Frau und Göttin: Exegetische und ikonographische Studien zum weiblichen Gottesbild im Alten Israel und in dessen Umwelt* (Göttingen).
Woolley, C. L. (1934), *Ur Excavations II: The Royal Cemetery* (London and Philadelphia).
—— (1952), *Carchemish III: The Excavations in the Inner Town* (London).
—— (1955), *Ur Excavations IV: The Early Periods* (London).
Woolley, C. L. & Mallowan, M. E. L. (1962), *Ur Excavations IX: The Neo-Babylonian and Persian Periods* (London and Philadelphia).
—— (1976) *Ur Excavations VII: The Old Babylonian Period* (London and Philadelphia).
Yadin, Y. *et al.* (1960), *Hazor* II (Jerusalem).
—— (1961), *Hazor III-IV (Plates)* (Jerusalem).
Young, J. H. & Young, S. H. (1955), *Terracotta Figurines from Kourion in Cyprus* (Philadelphia).
Zettler, R. L. (1996), 'Written documents as excavated artifacts and the holistic interpretation of the Mesopotamian archaeological record', in Cooper, J. S. & Schwartz, G. M. (eds.), *The Study of the Ancient Near East in the Twenty-First Century: The William Fox Albright Centennial Conference* (Eisenbraun: Winona Lake, Indiana), 81–101.
Ziffer, I. (1998), *O my Dove, that art in the clefts of the rock: The Dove-allegory in Antiquity* (Eretz Israel Museum, Jerusalem).

General Index

Abu Salabikh, Tell 20
Adam 11
Aegean Region 44
Afis, Tell 58
Ahlström, G.W. 62
Ain Ghazal 16–18
Akkadian Period 27–8
Albright, W.F. 7
Anat 64
Apollo, Sanctuary of 63
Arad 51
Architectural models, terracotta 21–2, 41–2, 64
Ashdod 65
Asherah 3–4, 5, 14, 27, 47–8, 55, 61, 64, 67
asherim 4, 49
"Ashdoda" figurines 64
Ashur-bel-kala, King of Assyria 32
Assur 33, 59–60
Assur-nasir-pal II, King of Assyria 31
Assyria 12–13, 33, 59–60
Astarte plaques 38–40

Baal 61, 64
Babylonia 11, 28–34
Babylonian Exile 67
Bachofen, J.J. 5–6
Bahrani, Z. 10–11, 32–3
Basle 5
baštu 33
Beck, P. 42
Beersheva 65
Beit Mirsim, Tell 57
Bellapais-Vounous 21–2
Bethel 51
Braudel, F. 14
Burchardt, J. 5

Canaan 1, 14–15, 22, 23, 25, 30–1, 35–40, 48, 51, 68
Caprids 64
Çatalhöyük 5
Cauvin, J. 6

Caves 52–8
Clay and creation 11–12
Collingwood, R.G. 6
Crowfoot, J.M. 52
Crown, horned 26–7
Cult objects 1–4
Cult stands, terracotta 41–2
Cultures, Samarra and Ubaid 19
Cylinder seals 31–2
Cyprus 21–2, 44, 48–9, 59, 61

Dan, Tell 51
Deity, concept of 17
Deer 64
Dever, W.G. 55
Dikaios, P. 21
Divided Monarchy 2
Dornemann, R.H. 61
Duweir, Tell ed- 7

Early Dynastic Period (Sumer) 25–7
Ebla (Tell Mardikh) 34
Edom 65
Egypt 25, 35–7
El 5, 48, 57, 61, 64
En Hazeva 65
Esdraelon, Plain of 43
Eshel, I. 53–4
Eustathius 21

Face-masks 17
Farah (North), Tell 58
Favissa 54
Fertility 10–11
Figurines, metal 14–15, 38, 48
Figurines, terracotta, animal 2, 13, 15, 17, 54, 63–4, 66
  Assyrian 11–13, 59–60
  anthropological approaches to 6–7
  Babylonian 11–13
  birds 64, 66

Figurines, terracotta, animal (*cont.*)
  breakage of 10, 17–18, 29, 52, 66–7
  building models 21–2, 41–2, 64
  Canaanite 2, 14, 37, 40–6
  categories 1–2, 6–7, 9–10
  columnar (see also Judean Pillar-
    Figurines) 27
  contexts 2
  disappearance of 67
  Egyptian 35–7
  female 2, 4–5, 23–45, 47–8, 53, 57–61
  fetishes 18
  furniture models 64
  inanimate 2, 64
  inscribed 12–13
  Israelite 15, 49–68
  male 14–15, 19–21, 38, 61–3
  musicians 44
  prehistoric legacy of 17
  Sumerian 25–7
  written references to 11–13
Foster, B. 11
Franken, H. 18, 53

Galilee 67
Gihon spring, Ophel (Jerusalem) 52
Gilbert-Peretz, D. 53
Gombrich, E.H. 14
Goddesses 13, 23–5, 47–9
Greece 5

Hadley, J. 4, 57
Hajji Firuz, Iran 6
Harness-trappings, bronze and ivory 43
Hathor 35–7
Hazor 63
Hebrew Bible 1
Holladay, J.S. XI
Holland, T. 54
Horses 42–3
Horse-riders 45, 61–3
Horvat Qitmit 42, 56, 65–6
"Hosts of Heaven" 61
Houses 2, 51
Huizinga, J. 8, 59

Idumea 67
Images 13–14
Inanna-Ishtar 26, 32, 34–5, 50
Incense burners 57
Iraq 19

Israel 1, 14, 22, 25, 50–1, 68
Israelite religion 1, 3–4
Ivory carvings 43, 60

Jar handles, anthropomorphic 26–7
Jericho 17
Jeroboam I 51
Jerusalem, "City of David" 53
  Ophel: Cave I 51–5
  Temple Mount 55
Judah 1, 4, 14, 15, 22, 43, 48, 50–1, 52–5,
  58–67, 68
Judea 67
Judean Pillar Figurines 4, 14, 48–9, 53,
  57–61

Kafr Kanna, Galilee 66
Kadesh-Banea, Sinai 3
Kassites 13
Keel, O. 8–9, 34
Kenyon, K.M. X, 7, 16, 52–4, 62
Khirbet el–Qom (nr. Hebron) 3, 47
Kidron Valley, Jerusalem 55
Kinyras 21
Kish, Iraq X, 20, 26–7, 33
Kletter, R. 4, 57–8, 60
Kourion, Cyprus 63
Kuntillet Ajrud, Sinai 3, 47

Lamps 57
Levi-Strauss, C. 18–19
Lion 64
Literature, Assyro-Babylonian 9
Lotus-flower 36–7, 38, 45

Magic 9–10, 45
Male Imagery 4, 19–21, 35, 38, 48, 50, 61,
  63
Mari 26
Mastuma 45
McAdam, E. 18
Mazzeboth 54
Meals, sacral 57
Mellaart, J. 5–6
Menelaos 21
Miniaturization 16
Mother-Goddess 5–6, 26
Moulds 14–15
Muhammad Diyab, Tell 41

GENERAL INDEX

Naram-Sin, King of Akkad 28
Nabu-apla-iddina, King of Babylon 31
Nasbeh, Tell en- 57
Neb 38
Nevali Çorî 19
Nietzsche, F. 5
Nineveh, Iraq 32
Nippur, Iraq 29
Nut 38

Old Testament 49–50
Oppenheim, A.L. 9, 30

Paphos, Cyprus 21
Patai, R. 5
Pella, Jordan 42
Philistines 43, 44, 64, 65, 67
Phoenicia 42, 44, 58–61, 65, 67
Pinch, G. 36
Plaques, terracotta, Babylonian, 28–30;
    Canaanite and Egyptian, 35–40;
    Canaanite legacy, 15, 40–6, 58;
    Syrian, 34, 45
Postgate, J.N. x, 13
Pottery 52–5, 56
Prag, K. 52–3
Pritchard, J. 2

Qos 65
Qudshu plaques 38–9, 43

Rassam, H. 30
Rehoboam, King of Judah 51
Reiner, E. 9
Religion, Israelite 1–2, 3–4
    polytheistic 9
Reyes, A. 48
Rifaʻat, Tell 59
Rome 5

Sabi Abyad, Tell 20
Samarra culture, Iraq 19, 25
Samaria 52, 55–8, 67

Sarepta, Lebanon 65
Schweich, L. ix, I
Sculpture, prehistoric 16–19
Seals 58
Sexuality 10–11
Shamash 30–1
Shar-kali-sharri, King 28
Shrines, terracotta models 41–2, 66
Sippar, Iraq 30–1
Skulls, human, plastered 16–17
Stands, terracotta 41–2, 53
Statuary, plaster, prehistoric 16–17
Storage jars 26
Sumer 20–1, 25–8
Sutians, Babylonia 31
Syria 34–5, 44–5, 48, 58, 61

Taanach, Tell 35, 42
Tadmor, M. 39
Tappy, R. 55
Teraphim 49
Terracottas (see under Figurines)
Texts, Mesopotamian 11–13
Thomas, K. 9
Toys 2, 7–8, 59
Transjordan 48, 61
Turkey 5

Ubaid Culture, Iraq 19, 25
Ucko, P.J. 6
Ugarit (Ras Shamra), Syria 5, 48
Underworld deities, 33
Ur, Iraq 20, 27, 29–30
Ur III Dynasty, Babylonia 28
Uruk 26

Van der Toorn, K. 23–5
Venus, planet 26
Voigt, M. 6, 8

Wiggerman, F.A.M. 33
Winter, U. 33–4

Yahweh 3–4, 11, 47, 50, 61, 64

Index of Biblical Passages

Genesis 2 : 7–8   11
Genesis 31 : 19   49
Deuteronomy 16 : 21   4
I Samuel 19 : 13–17   49
II *Kings* 23 : 4–7   55
II *Kings* 23 : 11   62

Isaiah 44 : 12–20   30
Jeremiah 7 : 18   50
Jeremiah 16 : 5   57
Jeremiah 44 : 19   49
Ezekiel 23 : 6–7, 23–4   62
Amos 6 : 7   57

ENNIS AND NANCY HAM LIBRARY
ROCHESTER COLLEGE
800 WEST AVON ROAD
ROCHESTER HILLS, MI 48307